New Beginning Presbyterian
# Church Library

This book
presented by

Wanda Biltz

Memorial Fund

AP

# Journey into Rest

## ELIZABETH SHERRILL

**BETHANY HOUSE PUBLISHERS**
MINNEAPOLIS, MINNESOTA 55438
A Ministry of Bethany Fellowship, Inc.

Material reprinted from *Daily Guideposts*, copyright © 1978, 1982, 1983, 1984, 1985, 1986, 1987, 1988, 1989 by Guideposts Associates, Inc., Carmel, NY 10512. Additional material copyright © 1990 by Elizabeth Sherrill.

Published by Bethany House Publishers
A Ministry of Bethany Fellowship, Inc.
6820 Auto Club Road, Minneapolis, Minnesota 55438

Printed in the United States of America

---

*Library of Congress Cataloging-in-Publication Data*

Sherrill, Elizabeth.
    Journey into rest / Elizabeth Sherrill.
        p.   cm.

    1. Voyages and travels—Religious aspects—Christianity—Meditations.  2. Devotional calendars.  3. Sherrill, Elizabeth.
I. Title.
BV4811.S377   1990
242'.3—dc20                          90–32103
ISBN 1–55661–133–1              CIP

*For John ...*
*who led the way ...*

ELIZABETH SHERRILL has published more than 1,000 magazine articles and has "ghosted" books, with sales in excess of 40 million, including *Our Christmas Story* (Mrs. Billy Graham), *Return From Tomorrow* (Dr. George Ritchie), and *Breaking Points* (the parents of John Hinckley). With her husband, John, she has coauthored *The Cross and the Switchblade*, *God's Smuggler*, *They Speak With Other Tongues*, *The Hiding Place*, *The Happiest People on Earth*, and *The Man Who Could Do No Wrong*.

The Sherrills met aboard ship on their way to Europe and were married in Geneva in 1947. For four years they traveled and free-lanced before joining the staff of *Guideposts* magazine in 1951. In 1970 they founded a publishing company dedicated to developing new Christian writers, *Chosen Books*, whose first title was Charles Colson's *Born Again*.

The Sherrills have three married children and six grandchildren. Their work has taken them on year-long writing assignments in Africa, South America, and Europe, as well as numerous trips to the Near and Far East. Elizabeth has conducted writing workshops on five continents.

# Contents

# *Invitation to a Spiritual Pilgrimage*

"*J*ourney into Rest" ... isn't this a contradiction? Is it movement or stillness that brings us to God? Effort or repose?

It is both, saints have answered through the centuries—and if this surprises us, that's as it should be.

For what a curious route it is, this pathway to God! Whether we've been following it for a lifetime, a year, or only since yesterday, all we can be sure of is that the unexpected awaits us around each bend.

Surprise is the hallmark of the pilgrim journey. To find ourselves embarked on it in the first place ... certainly this isn't our idea! The tug comes from outside ourselves; like Abraham we set forth without any idea where we are heading.

We encounter at once the second surprise. With that first tentative step, however hesitant, we're aware of another footfall keeping pace with our own. We are not traveling alone. We have a Companion on the way, closer than the staff in our hands or the sandals on our feet. It is Jesus who has called us to undertake this journey; Jesus who is the goal toward which we press; and Jesus, to our endless amazement, who becomes the Way we travel.

This is why pilgrims for two thousand years have reported the paradox:

Faith is to be a journey. Faith is to be at rest.

The mystery of stillness within movement is simply this: to begin is to be already at our goal. "All the way to heaven is heaven," wrote one traveler, "for He said, 'I am the Way.'" The path of faith is not a competitive course—with some runners near the finish line, others far behind. At every stage of the journey we are simultaneously living in the Promised Land. "Our feet are standing within thy gates, O Jerusalem," marveled the psalmist, and at each resting place along the way we see with wondering hearts that it is so.

### The Cloud of Witnesses

*Journey Into Rest* describes where some of these resting places have been for me. Each section begins as I begin every month: with the Scriptures, examining one of the epic journeys of the Bible. I've chosen our guides from that great "cloud of witnesses" invoked by the writer to the Hebrews. To this early Christian, the soul's progress was a kind of divine relay race, one generation passing the baton to the next until all of us together achieve the victory.

"Therefore," he concludes his list of heroes, "since we are surrounded by so great a cloud of witnesses ... let us run with perseverance the race that is set before us." (Heb.12:1)

These earlier travelers, in his concept, are to be a kind of coaching staff for our own stage of the journey—pioneers who've braved these deserts and detours ahead of us and will share with us the secrets of the road.

Aren't these great patriarchal figures too grand company for you and me? Didn't they move on a higher plain? Another surprise of this surprising journey is to discover just the opposite: these forerunners of our faith were fallible human beings. The last we see of righteous Noah, he is sprawled on his bed in a drunken stupor. Sublime Elisha sics wild bears on a group of children who poke fun at his bald pate.

Scripture makes no attempt to cover up these character flaws. On the contrary, it calls our attention to them. There can be only one hero in the Bible—God Himself. It is He who has called us on this journey, He who will see us safely to the end. "Let us run with perseverance ...," says the writer, "*looking to Jesus* the pioneer and perfecter of our faith."

Elizabeth Sherrill<br>
Chappaqua, New York

# Part I

# The Journey

*My Presence will go with you, and I will give you rest.*
*—Exodus 33:14*

*Setting Out:*

## Preparing for the Journey

# 1     *Traveling Companion:* *ABRAHAM* *... who stepped into the unknown*

> *Go from your country and your*
> *kindred and your father's house to the*
> *land that I will show you.*
>
> GENESIS 12:1

$G$od's marching orders to Abraham are the very ones He gives to you and me at the start of each year, each week, each day. "Leave the past behind. Venture with Me into territory you have not yet glimpsed!"

Leave behind old hurts and hates, old limitations. And leave the good as well: last year's insight, the truth that was so stretching yesterday. Dare for the better! Abraham's country and kindred were not evil—they were simply not all that God had in mind for him.

Where is God leading you now? You will know only by setting out. The *direction* was all God would show Abraham in the beginning, not the *destination*. The journey itself, the putting of one foot after the other in faith, is to be our great training ground in trust.

My husband John and I experienced this years ago in Africa. Our life as young parents in the suburbs of New York had not been wicked, only familiar. Within the routines of shopping at the supermarket and driving the kids to the dentist it was easy to forget our daily, hourly dependence on God. Not in Uganda! There we found ourselves praying over every food item, every turn on the unmarked jungle roads. Our need for God was no greater than it had always been; it was our awareness of that need which increased.

The same is true of the interior journey. As long as we cling to accustomed formulas, satisfied with what we already know of God, taking no risks with our faith, we will not experience that moment-by-moment "companionship of the way" God longs to provide.

What can we learn from Abraham as we set out on our journey?

*Oases*

The route to which God called Abraham was across arid plateaus and dry hill country. How would he water his sheep and goats and feed the men, women and children who depended on him?

By consulting caravan masters who had traveled this way ahead of him, planning each day's trek to end at an oasis.

From those who have gone ahead of us, we too can learn the importance of these times of refreshment. Scheduled quiet times, daily Bible reading, a home prayer group, and regular church attendance are a few of the ways seasoned travelers pace their journey.

### Nomad timing

We're on a *walk* of faith, not a jet flight dictated by a timetable. There is no schedule on our pilgrimage: Abraham paused or moved on as pasturage dictated. If one of the readings feeds you, stay with it! If a particular traveling companion has a lot to say to you, walk with him for two months, six months. Calendars were invented by settled agricultural societies; we are wayfarers, learning with nomadic Abraham to stay until the well runs dry.

### Altars

God's guidance to Abraham was progressive, revealed little by little as he "passed through the land." At each place where God's will, God's nature, God's purpose became clearer, "he built there an altar"—a place of worship marking the ground as holy. A "trip log" is one way of erecting altars along your personal route: a notebook in which to record insights, resolutions, thanksgiving.

*The unseen city*

Abraham died without ever reaching his final destination: "the city ... whose builder and maker is God." But he died in faith—not in disillusionment—"... not having received what was promised, but having seen it and greeted it from afar..." (Heb. 11:10, 13). Isn't this the essence of faith: confident affirmation of what is still—in our time frame—future tense?

The walk of faith is not for those who need quick results; it is for those for whom, for now, the journey in God's company is enough.

> *Keep thou my feet,*
> *I do not ask to see*
> *The distant scene;*
> *One step enough for me.*
> —*John Henry Newman*

*Lead me, LORD, one step at a time.*

## 2 *Angle of Repose*

*Return, O my soul, to your rest.*
PSALM 116:7

*I*'m a compulsive reader of plaques. I pull off
highways to read historical markers, stop before
signposts on nature trails. It makes travel slow and
walking non-aerobic, but over the years I've made
some lovely discoveries.

Beside a mountain stream in North Carolina a sign
calls attention to the slope of the banks. Their V-
shape, the plaque points out, can be wide or narrow
depending on the material the bank is made of. Solid
rock erodes to steep-sided banks, while softer soil
melts to a gentle slope. In either case, when the bank
no longer tumbles into the river with every passing
storm, it is said to have reached its "angle of repose."

Do people too, I wondered as I read that plaque,
have an angle of repose? Can we reach a place where
the storms of life no longer threaten our stability? In
the years since, I've watched this happen in the lives
around me: friends buffeted by illness, failure,
tragedy—standing firm in the love of God.

For every person the resting place is different. A Bible passage, a favorite hymn, a habit of prayer, a tradition of worship—for each of us it is the place where we find God's undergirding strength. When we rest in Him even as we journey—through downpour and drought, freeze and thaw—we have found the secret of travel that does not weary, movement that is fixed in Him.

*On this pilgrimage of faith,*
*LORD, teach me to rest in You.*

## 3      *Night Glow*

*Christ shall give you light.*
EPHESIANS 5:14

*J*ohn laughed when I bought the "Night Glo" slippers, but I liked the gimmicky things. Patches of specially treated cloth sewn to the insoles glowed in the dark; I no longer had to grope about for my slippers in the middle of the night.

They'd be especially helpful, I thought, for

travel—waking up in unfamiliar rooms. On our very next trip I brought them along.

In a hotel room one evening I took them out of the suitcase. The next morning, however, when I felt beside the bed in the predawn dark, not a glimmer guided me to where they lay somewhere beyond the reach of my hand. I said nothing to John as I packed them away; they were perfectly good slippers, even if I had paid extra for a patented feature that proved short-lived.

We'd been home several days when one black night I opened my eyes to see the pair of them gleaming cheerily at me from across the room. Why was the treated cloth working now, I wondered, when on the trip it had not?

On the bottom of the slippers themselves was the explanation: "To restore Night Glo, expose to light." In the closed suitcase they'd had no chance to store up their borrowed brightness.

I'm thinking of that little parable as I set out on this spiritual pilgrimage. When the glow goes out of the journey, when it's darkness all around me, when I see no glimmer of guidance—isn't it because I've shut myself away from daily, intimate communion with Him?

*Any time I can't find my way, LORD, let me rest for a season in Your light.*

# 4    *September Song*

> *He found nothing but leaves; for it was*
> *not the season for figs.*
>
> MARK 11:13

*I* was raking leaves one late September day when a small brown-backed bird with a spotted chest flitted out of the woods and just as swiftly darted back. A wood thrush. Not much to look at with his drab coloring: His glory is his song. On spring evenings he's a liquid voice from the forest edge, a flute song at twilight.

Not a sound did this one utter, of course—wrong time of year. Still, I gazed longingly into the trees where he had vanished, hoping in vain for some reprise of his rhapsody of four months ago, some thrush-style September song.

*What melody that small bird is endowed with,* I thought—and how parsimonious he is with his great gift, spending it on his narrow concerns of territory and mating, locked into his cycle of seasonal behavior.

*Do we humans, too, have neglected gifts,* I

wondered, *channeled by habit into narrow repetitive paths, clutched selfishly to our own small uses?* Is God even now looking longingly at His most gifted creation, telling us: "You could sing if you would!"

> *FATHER, I want to press toward Your kingdom, in season, out of season.*

5                    *The Key*

> *In the day of my trouble I call on thee, for thou dost answer me.*
> PSALM 86:7

*I* am seated before my new computer keyboard—with the trembling and apprehension that habitually seizes those of us who became grandparents before the age of micro chips. The motor hums with unexplored capabilities, while a blinking yellow dash line impatiently taps its electronic finger beneath the next blank space on the screen. Blank space is the most daunting thing a writer faces—

24

and this blank is alive and watching me....

But, oh, comfort in the midst of this technological wilderness! At the bottom of the screen is the message: F-1 HELP. And in the upper left-hand corner of the keyboard, sure enough, there's a key labeled "F-1." By pushing it I instantly bring up a whole screenful of explanations, reminders and instructions.

A key for help ... what a reassurance! Even though I can't yet grasp and utilize all the help available, I know that it is there.

Best of all ... that help holds for the new spiritual territory I'll be exploring, too: "F" for *Father*, "1" for *first*—whenever the complexities of the journey are great.

*FATHER. First.*

*Travelers' Advisory:*

## Assessing the Danger

# 6 Traveling Companion: CALEB ... who scouted the route

*Moses sent them to spy out the land of Canaan.*

NUMBERS 13:17

*T*he children of Israel were on the most daring journey any of us can make: out of slavery—whatever form it takes in our lives—into freedom. As they neared the end of the long trek across the wilderness, Moses sent twelve men ahead to report on the land to which they were headed. They were to bring back answers to six questions. Three had to do with the Promised Land (the incentive for making the journey):

1. Was the land good or bad?
2. Rich or poor?
3. Did it contain wood?

And three with the people presently living there

(the obstacles the travelers would encounter):

4.  Were the people strong or weak?
5.  Few or many?
6.  Did they live in camps or strongholds?

Those are the questions we who have embarked on a spiritual journey must answer too. What do we know of this promised Land of Rest?

1.  Will your reaching it be good news or bad news for others? (Will it increase your involvement in the world around you? Or make you passive and indifferent?)
2.  Will your own life in this land be richer or poorer? (Will you develop your gifts and uniqueness there? Or surrender your individuality?)
3.  Will the land supply all you need? Or will you have to import building materials from elsewhere?

And what about the resistance you will encounter—both interior, in the form of fears and doubts, and exterior, in the reactions of those close to you? Will the opposition be:

4.  Violent and traumatic, or easily overcome?
5.  Centered on only a few issues, or contesting every step of the way?
6.  Temporary, or deeply entrenched?

So the twelve scouts set out. After forty days spying out the green hills of Canaan, they returned to the wilderness camp and reported. All agreed on what they had seen. As for the land, it was infinitely worth possessing: "It flows with milk and honey!"

About the inhabitants the spies were also unanimous: "The people who dwell in the land are strong, the cities are fortified and very large." Not only were the opposing forces numerous and well entrenched, they were made up of giants! "All the people that we saw are men of great stature!"

This was the intelligence report—tantalizing and terrifying—that the advance party brought back. All twelve concurred on the facts. Two of the scouts— Caleb and Joshua—looked at these facts with eyes of faith: "Let us go at once and occupy it!" The other ten reacted to identical information with fear: "We are not able to go up against the people; for they are stronger than we."

"Fear is to the devil," someone has said, "what faith is to God." As God uses faith to make us strong, the devil uses fear to weaken and destroy. The fear-filled words of the ten soon had the entire people weeping in terror: "Let us go back to Egypt!" The devil of fear had done his work; the children of Israel were condemned to forty years of homeless wandering.

Faith versus fear! We long for more of one, less of the other—but how? All twelve spies were handpicked for courage. What made ten see giants, two opportunity?

The key is not *what* the scouts saw, but *where* they stood while they looked. The viewpoint, not the view, made the difference.

"We seemed to ourselves like grasshoppers," reported the ten. That's the view from the human perspective, obstacles seen from the standpoint of our own weakness—an insect's-eye view of the situation.

"And so we seemed to them." That's the view through the eyes of the enemy. The Israeli spies could not really have known how the inhabitants of Canaan were reacting in their own hearts. But they looked up at them (so huge!) and read contempt in their bearing (they'll only laugh at us!). They gave the devil more than his due, imagined a far stiffer resistance than in fact ever developed.

Caleb, on the other hand, envisioned the scene through God's eyes. Rejecting the picture painted either from the vantage point of our puny selves or of our powerful-seeming enemies, Caleb focused on the all-sufficiency of God: "If the Lord delights in us, he will bring us into this land and give it to us."

Ask yourself right now: Where am I standing as I survey the road to all that God has promised? On my own merits? Or on the high ground of His purposes, His desire for me?

Caleb chose that high ground. When we meet

him next, in the book of Joshua, he is an old man, sole survivor, with Joshua, of their entire generation: "The Lord has kept me alive, as he said, these forty-five years ... while Israel walked in the wilderness; and now, lo, I am this day eighty-five years old. I am still as strong to this day as I was in the day that Moses sent me.

"So now," he says to Joshua, his old fellow scout, "give me this hill country"—the land the two had reconnoitered so long ago. It has still to be wrested from the powerful people living there, but Caleb refuses to shift his attention to the impediments: "It may be that the Lord will be with me, and I shall drive them out."

And with God's help, Caleb did.

*FATHER, give me Your perspective on the trials of the road ahead.*

7 *Mirror Image*

*Our wives and our little ones will
become a prey; would it not be better
for us to go back to Egypt?*
NUMBERS 14:3

*L*ast spring a robin abandoned his nest site in the dogwood tree behind our house ... because of an enemy who did not exist. I became aware of his desperate shadow-war when he hurled himself at the kitchen window with a bang that brought me running to see what pot had dropped from the wall.

Stunned, the robin sat on the sill for a while, then returned to the attack, flinging himself over and over at the glass. What he was battling, of course, was his own reflection: a bird as pugnacious and tireless as himself. I tried draping towels over the window to block the mirror-effect; it only changed the site of hostilities. A score of times a day I'd hear his frantic flapping—up in the bedroom, down in my study—kept from his constructive tasks by that imagined foe.

It started me thinking about the things that keep

*me* from making better progress. How many are actual threats from outside, how many reflections of something in me ... anger, guilt, some carry-over from childhood? Were those inhabitants of Canaan really such formidable folk, or did the Israelite scouts see a projection of their own self-doubt? Are other people trying to take advantage of me, or is it my own greed I read into their actions?

> *FATHER, show me if the obstacle in the road today is real—or simply my own shadow on the path.*

# 8      *Catch Basin*

> *Gather up the fragments ... that nothing be lost.*
> JOHN 6:12

*T*he Texas cattle ranch where John and I spent two months one fall was not what western movies had led me to expect. Giant oaks and scarlet sweet gums sheltered the mobile home that friends had provided as a hideaway. Most surprising to my Easterner's stereotype was a chain of tiny sparkling lakes alive with fish, home to ducks and herons.

"I didn't know," I said to John, "that Texas had this much water."

Nor, in fact, did it. Looking closer we saw that each little lake was actually a reservoir. An earthen dam had blocked some almost invisible rivulet, backing up and storing the precious water until the trickle that would otherwise soon have disappeared back into the parched ground had become a living lake, kept sweet by the fish that stocked it. During the dry season, the rancher told us, these man-made lakes provided the drinking supply for the thirsty cattle.

Not *man-made*, I thought, *man-preserved*. The rancher hadn't created the water, only known how to retain and make use of it. Wasn't there a lesson here for all of us whose journey leads through desert places: an invitation to better stewardship of God's provision? Not just the big things—the blessings of health, friends, family—but the small moment-by-moment mercies that all too soon disappear beneath the conscious surface.

It was the nudge that started me keeping a spiritual diary—a kind of catch basin of fleeting experiences that might otherwise be forgotten. "Bring back some of the fruit of the land," Moses instructed the scouts he sent into Canaan. Moses hoped the sight of juicy ripe grapes would put hope into the desert-weary multitude. It didn't; the rumored terrors outweighed the promise of the grapes. But the principle is a good one. When the journey is hard, how badly we need a foretaste of the good things awaiting us!

In my trip log a section is labeled "Fruit of the Land." Here I jot down instances of unexpected supply, sudden insight, providential timing, no matter how trivial or insignificant-seeming the event. These are tokens of life in the Promised Land: Stored and accumulated they form a reservoir of faith against the times when belief is hard.

*Show me yourself, LORD, in the small events of each day's journey.*

# 9      *Trust*

*Behold, I am doing a new thing . . .*
ISAIAH 43:19

*I* saw the small brown frog a moment before he vanished. Down into the mud he burrowed at my approach. Even though I knelt on the marshy ground and scanned the spot where he had been, not even a rising bubble betrayed his hiding place.

How wonderful, I thought as I resumed my walk. All of creation, it seems, has some special defense mechanism to call on in moments of danger. A little farther on, however, I encountered a second frog, and this time his defensive maneuver was not so successful.

Beside the road a section of concrete pipe some two and a half feet in diameter had been sunk vertically into the ground until the upper end was nearly flush with the surrounding land.

Peering down into it, I saw a frog of the same brown variety as the first one, sitting half in, half out of the puddle of water that had formed at the bottom, perhaps three feet down. Obviously, he had jumped unwarily in. Just as obviously, he could never leap three feet straight up to freedom. If I leaned down into the pipe, however, I could just reach him.

Slowly, slowly I lowered my hand to him. He watched me uneasily, sides swelling and falling. Another two inches and I could lift the captive creature out.

The next second he had burrowed into the mud. Calling on the instinct that had saved countless generations of his forebears, he dug instead to his doom. I waited a long while, but he did not reappear.

A frog, of course, has nothing to draw on in time of need except the approach that has worked in the past. God has given us too a set of survival tools: fear, on occasion anger, a little healthy suspicion, the ability to foresee difficulties. But He has also given us the capacity to hear His voice calling us to new responses. Calling us to new and radical trust as He lifts us from the prison of the past.

*LORD, I don't want to rely so blindly on old solutions that I fail to recognize Your gracious hand stretched out to me today. Show me the places where I'm burying myself in the mud rather than risking Your route to freedom.*

*Hearing God:*

*Getting Our Marching Orders*

# 10 Traveling Companion: SAMUEL
## ... who listened as he walked

*Speak, LORD, for thy servant hears.*
1 SAMUEL 3:9

*H*e was a circuit judge, tramping endlessly between district seats: from Bethel to Gilgal to Mizpah, then back to his wife and children in Ramah. Times were hard in Samuel's day. The Philistines, supplied with arms by Egypt, had driven the dispirited Israelites from the good bottomland; all they retained of the Promised Land were these rocky and infertile hills where Samuel walked.

His route took him regularly past the ruins of Shiloh, the town where he'd lived as a boy, razed to the ground during the Philistine occupation. That heap of rubble there had been the temple where the ark of the Lord had once been kept.

There was the gate—the only part of the wall still intact—where the old priest Eli used to sit.

Here Samuel's astonishing career had begun.

The sunburnt man trudging these stony hills was far more than an arbitrator of boundary disputes between farmers. He was a patriot who had roused his countrymen to throw off the Philistine yoke. He had summoned Israel away from idol worship, anointed kings and paved the way for the glorious period of Jewish history soon to follow.

It all began here in Shiloh early one morning before daylight, when twelve-year-old Samuel learned the secrets of hearing God . . .

## 1. Expect Him to speak

The youngster was awakened by a voice in the cold predawn. Jumping from his mat on the floor, he ran to Eli's side: "Here I am, for you called me."

But Eli had not called. Samuel returned to his pallet and the voice called again. Once more Samuel went to see what Eli wanted; once more he was told to go back to sleep. Yet a third time the urgent voice summoned him; still it never entered Samuel's head that he could be hearing God.

To me, this is an immensely reassuring story. I tend to imagine that the spiritual giants of the past had an easier time discerning God's voice than I do. But they were as hindered by their preconceptions as we are. If we do not—not *really*—expect God to speak, we will miss Him when He does.

## 2. Listen for your name

"Samuel! Samuel!" called the voice in Shiloh. In the Bible, a person's name stands for his uniqueness, the essential qualities that make him himself and no one else. God's word for the present moment always has a name attached. It is not only *logos*—true for all time and people—but *rhema,* true today for you in particular. It will speak in terms of what interests, distresses, frightens or delights you at this moment; it will "have your name on it."

## 3. Listen with your walking staff in your hand

To believe that God speaks, and speaks to you personally, is still not the whole story. When Samuel appeared a third time at Eli's bedside, the old priest realized that the lad was hearing God.

"If it happens again," he told the boy, "reply, 'Your servant is listening!' "

Not "your curious bystander is listening," or "your skeptic is waiting to be shown," or even "your scholarly investigator." Your *servant,* ready and waiting to do Your will—as soon as he knows what it is! When we present ourselves to God as servants, we offer our obedience, not our opinions. In Samuel's own view, years later, Jesse's tall, manly looking son Eliab was the right choice for king of Israel. But God, whose servant Samuel was, ordered him to anoint Jesse's youngest son, David. We engage to carry out God's design; only then does He unfold it for us.

## 4. Act on what you hear

"Your servant hears" was easy enough for young Samuel to say, but the message that followed pinned him to his mat in consternation. Could he be hearing right? Was he really to tell his venerable and beloved master that he and his entire family were going to be destroyed by God?

The boy obeyed: He passed on the fateful message. He must have remembered this moment of difficult obedience years afterward when he was instructed by the same divine voice to go to King Saul—Saul with his hair-trigger temper and killing rages—and inform him that God was wrenching the kingdom of Israel out of his hands.

Expectation, recognition, willingness, obedience—this is how we too receive directions for each day's journeying.

*LORD, let me learn with faithful Samuel to say, "Your servant hears."*

## 11 *Dependence*

*Therefore let any one who thinks that
he stands take heed lest he fall.*
1 CORINTHIANS 10:12

*I* went over the directions to Kennedy Airport one
more time as my friend climbed into her rented car.
It had been Elsa's first trip east since her husband's
death. Now she was returning home to Illinois after
visiting friends all over New England.

"And I haven't gotten lost even once!" she
marveled as she started the engine. On the seat
beside her was one reason: detailed directions to
each destination carefully written out ahead of time.

But there was a more important reason. "I've
prayed over every mile of this trip," she confided.
"I've asked God to help me find every route
number, every street sign."

I breathed a prayer too as she set off: Getting to
Kennedy from our home fifty miles north of New
York City is confusing even when you do it often.
Sure enough, that night Elsa phoned to say she'd
lost her way.

"And missed your flight!"

"Oh no," she said. Praying "like mad," she'd gotten to Kennedy just fine. It was later that the trouble came—after picking up her own car at O'Hare Airport in Chicago and heading out on a highway she'd driven all her life. She'd missed a crucial turn and gone fifteen miles out of her way.

"I was sure of myself," she explained. "So I stopped praying."

*Sometimes, LORD, I too get thinking I know the way. Remind me to ask directions of You, each step I take.*

## 12        *Roadblock*

*But the man of God sent word to the king of Israel, "Beware that you do not pass this place."*
2 KINGS 6:9

*I*t seemed like the last straw when the railroad-crossing barrier lowered just as I approached the tracks. All week there'd been delays that interfered with a writing deadline. Now I barely had time to get the finished manuscript to the post office before it closed. No train was in sight, but with flashing lights and ringing bells the barrier blocked my car from passing. I sat fuming. I'd certainly miss the last mail pickup now!

The train roared into view around the bend, looming suddenly a few feet from my front fender. *Big!* I thought, gaping up at it. Overpowering—all metal and speed and noise. I wouldn't want to be on the track when that thing arrived.

What had saved me from such a disaster? It was that barrier blocking the crossing, the one I'd been so annoyed at when it interrupted my all-important schedule.

Then I thought of the other impediments this week …

What if—just suppose—all these delays had not been casual bits of bad luck, but barriers lowered by a merciful, all-seeing God to prevent my rushing into a situation I was unaware of?

The final car of the train flashed past. The lights ceased blinking, the barrier lifted. I drove, slowly, across the tracks, found a place to turn around and headed home, determined to take a closer look at that manuscript. Was there something about it that wasn't right? (In fact, a call came the following day that postponed the publishing of that story for two years.)

I had no answers as I drove home, only a question that had not occurred to me before. One I hoped I would ask the next time I encountered an obstacle in my path.

*FATHER, is this frustration today a setback ... or a signal?*

13          *Listening*

*Let me hear what God the Lord will speak.*
PSALM 85:8

*T*he woman at the next table was obviously expecting someone—whirling around each time the door to the coffee shop opened. At last her friend joined her.

"I hated to call you at work, Ethel," the first woman plunged in, "but I need your advice."

Soon I, and everyone for several tables around,

were learning—willing or not—about the woman's problems. Clearly she had more of them than anyone could be expected to handle alone. An alcoholic husband, a delinquent son, a diabetic condition of her own ... the doleful list went on.

I found myself covertly studying Ethel's face. Warm, responsive, intelligent. I listened expectantly for the wisdom I was confident Ethel would supply.

"I wonder, Sue," she began, "if you've thought about—"

But Sue had launched into another melancholy story of disappointment and betrayal. And so it went, the older woman unable to break into the stream of words. I could almost see Ethel give up the effort to communicate. The last thing I heard as I rose to leave was Sue's distressed voice, "I just wish I knew what to do!"

I stepped outside thinking of the last time *I* had said those words—that very morning—not to an older, wiser friend, but to God. "Why don't You give me an answer!"

*Maybe,* I thought, *He's been trying.* Maybe my own voice has been so loud and insistent that the two-way conversation called prayer never had a chance.

*Lord, it's Your turn now.*

*Receiving Our
Equipment:*

# God's
# Provision for
# the Journey

# 14 Traveling Companion
## GIDEON
## ... who was stronger than he knew

*Go in this might of yours.*
JUDGES 6:14

*I*n 1898 two traveling salesmen stopping in the same hotel in Wisconsin got to discussing problems common to every traveler. Loneliness. Uncertainty. Temptation. Out of this chance meeting grew the organization known as The Gideons, which places "Gideon Bibles" in hotel rooms around the world—making the name Gideon synonymous with travel.

But who was Gideon?

When we meet him first, he is a timid young farmer living at a dismal moment in the history of the fledgling nation of Israel. The chosen people have established a foothold in the Promised Land— but their scattered settlements in the Canaanite Hills are far from secure. Bands of nomads sweep in off the desert, strike the settled communities, and vanish again into the wilderness.

In Gideon's time, the twelfth century B.C., these sporadic raids have assumed a new and terrifying dimension. As in our day, technology has made one of its sudden leaps, leaving people bewildered and demoralized. The Midianites, a tribe of nomadic Bedouins, have invented camel warfare, swifter and more unpredictable than anything yet known. Against these attacks there is no known defense ... except to flee to the mountains and hide.

The invaders, "like locusts for numbers," camp on the Israeli farms for a few weeks, devour everything in sight, then move on "and leave no sustenance in Israel, and no sheep or ox or ass."

Then Gideon and the other farmers creep down from their mountain hideaways to start again from scratch ... pulling their own plows for lack of draft animals ... re-staking the trampled vineyards—until at harvest time the whirlwind attack comes again.

"And Israel was brought very low because of Midian; and the people of Israel cried for help to the LORD."

First things reached rock bottom; *then* they turned to God. What the alcoholic, the gambler, the overeater—anyone at the mercy of "Midian"— eventually discovers is that his own strategies don't work. Alcoholics Anonymous and the programs copied after it *do* work. That is because their starting point is the admission: "I am powerless to help myself."

God's response to the Israelites' cry is to send instructions to Gideon through an angel. But Gideon doesn't believe that the stranger sitting under the oak tree comes from God, any more than we recognize the various guises in which He appears to us. It must be some newcomer who's never seen an armed camel rider and doesn't appreciate our situation.

Because what this ill-informed visitor is saying makes absolutely no sense: "The LORD is with you, you mighty man of valor."

*The LORD is with me?*

Our response is apt to be Gideon's: "Pray, sir, if the Lord is with us, why then has all this befallen us?" Why is my child sick? Why am I out of work?

*Me, a mighty man of valor?*

Valor is not exactly Gideon's hallmark. At the very moment that this preposterous greeting comes to him he is hiding from the Midianites at the bottom of a wine press. "My clan is the weakest in Manasseh," he whimpers, "and I am the least in my family."

But the angel continues: Gideon is to tear down the local pagan shrine. The young man obeys all right ... but after dark "because he was too afraid of his family and the men of the town to do it by day."

And this is the man God is going to send against a camel corps?

Yes: "Go in this might of yours and deliver Israel from the hand of Midian."

This might of Gideon's ... of yours and mine. A might we do not know we have, and therefore cannot use, until God shows it to us.

A contemporary to whom this happened is Terry Law. Incredibly to those who know him today, Terry was a shy Canadian college student—a "born loser" in his own eyes—when he came upon the story of Gideon. Struck by the change in the frightened young Israeli farmer, Terry began to use the Bible in a new way. He'd always known he could find God described there. Now he began to ask also: How does the Bible describe *me* as a child of God?

And there he was, Terry Law, unbelievably but unmistakably! Perfect. Victorious. Beloved. Tireless. Invincible. Blameless. Terry began to read the Bible daily, not only to get to know God better, but to become acquainted with himself as God saw him. Today Terry heads a worldwide outreach to communist countries, operating through direct confrontation with hostile authorities.

At the start of each day, ask God to give you a special word that describes you as you appear to Him. He may speak through another person, through something you read, or directly to your spirit. Will He call you *courageous*? *upright*?

*beautiful*? However it wars with your own self-concept, accept it as true in Him; then live the rest of the day as though it were perfectly realized in you.

"A sword for the Lord and for Gideon!" This was the rallying cry that aroused the victimized Israelites to go on the offensive against Midian. Before long, 32,000 men had assembled. But "the Lord said to Gideon, 'The people with you are too many for me to give the Midianites into their hand, lest Israel vaunt themselves against me, saying, "My own hand has delivered me." ' "

God wants there to be no mistake about where the strength comes from. He wants us confident, not cocky; valiant, but not vain. And so He instructed Gideon to send all but 300 men back to their homes. With this handful He—and valorous Gideon—ended the Midianite scourge forever.

*Thank You, LORD, for the assets You have given me. I accept them as Your perfect provision for the road ahead.*

# 15 *Front Room*

*Every good endowment and every
perfect gift is from above.*
JAMES 1:17

*I*t was after dark when we arrived at the shore.

"Nothing's going to be open here this time of year," John warned.

Something had come over us after months of winter ... a longing to hear ocean waves and sniff salt air. And so we'd jumped into the car, driven to the nearest seashore—the coast of New Jersey—to try to find a place on the water to spend the night. But we'd driven through one seaside town after another without finding so much as a gas station open. Then, as we were about to give up, we spotted it—a small sign in front of a turreted Victorian mansion. "Open All Year." Soon we were being shown up a carved oak stairway to a high-ceilinged room with a four-poster bed. Lulled by the sound of waves, we drifted to a peaceful sleep.

The next morning, we found the young owner vacuuming the room next to ours. "I'm sorry I didn't have this one ready last night," she said. "It's our biggest room."

It was big, all right. Twice the size of the one we'd had, with windows on three sides, and a choice collection of period furniture. And somehow as we strolled on the beach, the warmth had gone from the winter sun.

"It's because of that front room, isn't it?" John said. And of course as soon as he said it we saw the childishness of it. We who'd been given the sea and the sun were out of sorts because we couldn't have the moon too!

That little episode taught me something. I'd always thought the opposite of gratitude was ingratitude. It's not. The opposite of gratitude is greed. Taking our eyes off God and His moment-by-moment provision for us, and fixing them on what looks bigger, better, more desirable.

Whenever we wish He had given us something different from what we've received, we are not letting God be God ... and ourselves be loved.

*Thank You, FATHER, for just what You give today.*

# 16 *Supply*

*[God] is able to do far more
abundantly than all that we ask or
think.*

EPHESIANS 3:20

When I first saw the running faucet I wanted to turn it off.

The faucet is on the end of a pipe bringing water down from the hills to a horse trough outside the village of Endorf, Germany. It's an ordinary spigot, just like the tap over our kitchen sink at home—only this one can't be turned off. It runs continually, day and night, water gushing ceaselessly from its metal nozzle, spilling over the stone sides of the trough into a ditch.

At first, as I say, I wanted to stop it, to stem the waste, to block that continuous pouring-out. Then the faucet began to speak to me. *There's plenty of water in these hills, it said. More than anyone could ever use. I'm drawing on God's limitless supply to fill this trough—but because I'm only a household fixture, you can't believe in such abundance.*

That's it, you see. I know about God's infinite riches in nature. Thundering waterfalls, rushing rivers, springs bubbling up out of the ground— these don't fill me with fears of the water running out.

But to see that supply in personal terms? In the familiar and the commonplace? To apply that abundance to my daily need? I come out to this horse trough often now. I sit on the stone wall and I let that faucet tell me: There's more than you'll ever need.

*FATHER, I'm afraid of not having enough strength for the journey: enough money, enough time, enough skill. Today, let Your abundance speak to my fear.*

# 17 *Pecan Tree*

*My cup overflows.*
PSALM 23:5

*U*p by the road, during our stay in Texas, there was a huge old tree where I'd often see a car or a truck pulled over, people picking up something from the ground. I went to look.

Pecans!

It was the first pecan tree I'd ever seen. Pecans come in cellophane packages on the grocery shelf; they don't lie about for the taking. But morning after morning the ground beneath the tree would yield eight, ten, a dozen. To me it became a daily renewed miracle literally dropping from above. I'd start my early walk in that direction before the night's windfall could be collected by someone else.

I was dismayed, therefore, one morning to find a whole group of people there ahead of me, half a dozen teenagers running, stooping, combing the ground, while others scrambled through the branches of my tree. No use even looking, with so much competition. I turned away, resolving to come an hour earlier the next day, when a hallo from high in the tree stopped me.

"Hey, lady! Want some pecans?"

Another boy, one of those who'd been gathering the rain of nuts from the branch-shakers, ran up to me with a sack of them. Not the handful I'd been gathering, but a grocery bag filled to the top. "Here, we've got more than we can use."

"Don't you know," I could almost hear God saying, "that I have more than enough for all?" I did know. It was just that I'd starting thinking of that tree as mine. It took a bunch of kids to remind me that it was His.

*LORD, I'm so grateful it's Your tree, Your world of infinite supply.*

*Trailblazers:*

*Learning
From Those
Who've Gone
Before*

# 18 Traveling Companion: ELISHA
## ... who walked behind another

*Then he arose and went after Elijah.*
1 KINGS 19:21

*H*e counseled kings, he raised the dead, he fed multitudes with a few loaves of bread. But when I think of Elisha it is not first of all as the bald-headed wonder worker he later became. It is as a young man ... following in the footsteps of another. There are two figures on the heat-shimmering roads of Palestine, and Elisha's is second. A few steps ahead of him strides Elijah, Elisha's teacher and guide. It's a relationship that suggests our own need for pathfinders on our spiritual journey.

Our guide may be a contemporary—a famous preacher, some saint living down the block. Or someone we know through books—Albert Scheitzer or St. Teresa. Maybe one pacesetter will guide our journey from start to finish, as Francis of

Assisi did for St. Clare. Or maybe at each stage in our pilgrimage a new companion will point the way. Whenever and however theses heroes appear, one thing is sure: our lives are never again the same.

This is certainly how it was for young Elisha, plodding peacefully along behind his ox team, when a gaunt, travel-stained stranger strode across his field. Elisha's farm lay in the loveliest part of Palestine, the fertile valley south of the Sea of Galilee. The family home would have been a rambling kilned-brick building with a stucco facade and an interior of cool limestone. Here in this pleasant setting Elisha expected to live out his days.

## Step 1: Finding our roots

Barring war or other disaster, only one thing could upset this gratifying life plan. Only one thing can shake you and me loose from our comfortable pattern and set us marching for God.

That is the vision of our place in a larger story. We may be sure Elisha had this vision simply because he was a Hebrew. At about five he would have joined the other boys of the village to begin his study of history, absorbing the God-haunted saga of his people from the elders of his community. That sacred history is our story too.

## Step 2: Hearing the call

Now grown up, with his own snug slot in the scheme of things, Elisha is pursuing the work he has always done. And suddenly, in the very act of turning a furrow—putting the dishes in the dishwasher, typing a paper for school, boarding the train for work—he feels an unfamiliar mantle settle over his shoulders. That God has a purpose for human life, that He has acted through individual people in the past—this we can learn through study. But to believe that He wants to act *now*—and through *me*—that takes a personal encounter.

How and when do we receive this personal directive? Probably it will *not* come, as it did not for Elisha, while we are sitting with our hands folded awaiting a message-from-on-high, but while we are going energetically about our daily tasks.

*Step 3: Counting the cost*

The meaning of the great prophet's gesture was clear at once to Elisha. Clear and terrifying: Someday *you* are to wear my cloak—to "fill my shoes," we would say today. Elisha the farmer succeed the famous prophet Elijah? Elisha recognized him of course—all Israel knew the great man who in a showdown with the prophets of Baal only a few weeks previously had called down fire from heaven!

Whatever calling you and I have from God, it can scarcely be more daunting than Elisha's. Daunting and—humanly speaking—unwelcome. Leave the bulging barns of home for a life of conflict and risk? Ever since King Ahab married the foreign princess Jezebel, Elijah has carried on a one-man-protest campaign against her religion. At this very moment he is the object of an official manhunt.

*Step 4: Giving our answer*

Elisha, however, needs no persuading. Just as a group of fishermen on the nearby lake, hundreds of years in the future, will respond to another call and leave their nets, so Elisha drops his plow without even finishing the field.

Elijah meanwhile has not even broken his stride. The old prophet is already on his way; Elisha has to run after him with his resounding "Yes!" Elisha knows how very much he has to learn. He knows he will not have a day, not an hour too much with his companion on the road. As swiftly as that he makes the transition from a landowner, a man with his own plans and expectations, to a disciple, a follower of another.

> *Thank You, LORD, for the pioneers of our faith. Show me the guide You've chosen for me—and give me the grace to set out running!*

# 19                    *Seeing*

*Who can show forth all his praise?*
PSALM 106:2

*F*rom the windows of the apartment we rented while working in Austria, John and I could see the mountain called the Hochkoenig.

That is, we could sometimes see it. Mists rising from the valley often hid it altogether. Other days just the snow-clad summit might appear. Or the top of the mountain would be cloaked in clouds while sun shone on the forested slopes.

No two glimpses of the Hochkoenig were alike. The light shifted constantly, highlighting at one moment a rocky ridge, in the next the silver thread of a waterfall. And of course even on the clearest day we could see only the mountainside that faced our valley.

Our German-English dictionary translated "Hochkoenig" as the "High King." And indeed our view of Hochkoenig was a little like our view of God. We know the High King is there, even when clouds obscure our vision. Different aspects of His inexhaustible reality come into focus for us at different seasons. Sometimes it's His majesty we see clearest. Other times His fatherhood, or His forgiveness. There are awe-struck moments when we seem to grasp the entire great sweep of His providence. And yet travelers from other valleys report heights and depths we've never glimpsed.

*Thank You, LORD, for what I see of You today. And thank You for the witness of those who've seen more.*

20      *First Impression*

*But seek first his kingdom....*
MATTHEW 6:33

*I* found a dime as I walked along a country road this afternoon. I stooped down and picked it up. A few yards away something else glinted in the bright sun. I detoured to look—only a bottle cap. Nearby was the ring-tab from a soft-drink can; several steps farther on, a foil gum wrapper glistening like silver.

I'd allowed myself half an hour away from my typewriter, and so after fifteen minutes I turned around. In that quarter-hour I'd seen a lot of litter and developed a crick in my neck from staring at the ground. One thing was sure, anyhow: there were no more coins beside the road.

So I raised my eyes as I headed back ... and saw a shaft of light on a gray stone wall, a nuthatch spiraling down a tree, maple leaves scarlet against a rough brown trunk.

What we look for determines what we find. I knew that. But I learned something more today. What we find at the *start* of a walk, a job, a new acquaintance is what we're apt to go on looking for the rest of that walk, that work, that relationship.

*Let me catch a glimpse of You, LORD, at the beginning of each new day.*

## 21        *Benches*

> *Thus says the LORD: "Stand by the*
> *roads, and look."*
> JEREMIAH 6:16

Walking in Europe, you come to benches
everywhere. Not only in parks, but along city streets
and country roads, in farmers' fields and on forest
paths.

Sometimes the bench bears the name of a
township or the initials of a hiking club; other times
there is no clue as to who has provided it. But
always the bench issues an invitation: *Stop! Pause.*
*Rest.*

I've tried to learn the lesson of the benches. At
first I thought it was simply that I was to slow down.
We're such hurriers, we Americans. Benches remind
us that we don't need to rush through the days.

But they do more. They tell us something about
the purpose of journeying. Why, I started asking, is
there a bench in this particular location?

There was always an answer. A spire framed
between rooftops. An ancient beech tree in a field.

A gap between hills allowing a glimpse of higher mountains beyond. Something I would have missed if the bench placer had not helped me see it.

That's the true message of the bench. It tells us, *Stop! Somebody saw beauty right here! Don't hurry so fast to reach some far-off goal that you overlook what's here at hand.*

> FATHER, *there will be benches along my path today. Let me learn from earlier travelers to rejoice in You right here, right now.*

*The Reluctant Traveler:*

*When We Don't Want to Go*

## 22 *Traveling Companion:* JONAH *... who ran in the opposite direction*

*But Jonah rose to flee to Tarshish from the presence of the Lord.*

JONAH 1:3

$A$braham, Caleb, Elisha—men given difficult roads to travel, who strapped on their sandals and set forth in faith. They make inspiring companions.

But I feel more comfortable with Jonah. Jonah took one look at the journey God was sending *him* on—and ran the other way. Told to travel northeast from his home in Galilee to the city of Nineveh on the Tigris River, he headed instead southwest—to Joppa on the Mediterranean. Once there, taking no chances, he found a ship and headed as far from Nineveh as possible: to Spain—the absolute limits of the known world.

Jonah went aboard, climbed into his bunk, and doubtless pulled the covers over his head. It was probably the loudest "No way!" ever uttered to a command of God, and it shows me a lot about myself. Jonah was to discover, as I do each time, the truth of the psalmist's words:

*If I take the wings of the morning*
*and dwell in the uttermost parts of the sea,*
*even there thy hand shall lead me,*
*and thy right hand shall hold me.*
                                    *—Psalm 139:9, 10*

How does God lead us, even in the midst of our disobedience? Jonah discovered four ways.

## 1. Storms

Uproar and confusion in our environment are often the external signs that we're headed the wrong direction. The truth which Jonah's story dramatizes is that everyone around us, even the innocent and uninvolved, is caught up in the turmoil brought about by our rebellion. An employee who fails to do his job, a volunteer who takes on a task intended for someone else make it impossible for others to fulfill *their* guidance. Jonah's "no" cost the ship's crew their cargo and very nearly their lives.

## 2. Man overboard

Jonah's flight from God brought him where it brings us all: over our heads in deep water. Each of us has his own method of avoiding God's claim on our lives, whether it's the 14-hour day of the workaholic, or the TV addiction of the escapist.

But sooner or later such dodges fail. The very ship we counted on to carry us to safety casts us out. Our health breaks down, reality closes in. Whatever the particular crisis, we find ourselves sinking beneath the waves. But the dunking is for our benefit. God wants us out of the boat so that we can enter into relationship with Him. As the water closed over Jonah's head then "I remembered the Lord" (Jonah 2:7).

### 3. The fish

Jonah, humanly speaking, was done for. But human resources are not the last word. When we come to the end of ours, God's are only beginning.

Who could have imagined, in Jonah's adversity, an enormous fish arriving and swallowing him up—a fish with a belly large enough for a man to live in! Who can imagine the means He will use in *your* predicament? All we can be sure of about His provision is that it will surprise us.

### 4. Landfall

Traveling the long way around, Jonah ends up back where he started. But of course it isn't really the same place. The shore where the great fish deposited Jonah was a lot farther from Nineveh than his original starting point in Galilee. His disobedience means that he has a longer road to go. As he trudges ruefully along, he must reflect that had he followed directions in the first place he would have been there by now.

But Jonah didn't obey right away, and neither, much of the time, do we. We are all of us to some degree off His perfect course for our lives. The great news of Jonah is that we can never stray so far that God cannot bring us back.

*Thank You, LORD, that when I run from Your purpose, You have already prepared the way to return.*

## 23 *Helen*

*O taste and see that the LORD is good!*
PSALM 34:8

*L*ong ago I learned something about the roads we don't want to take....

Of all the girls in my high-school homeroom, Helen was the one I liked least. And, of course, I drew her name for the class party. How to choose a gift for someone you knew nothing about and cared less....

I could always give her perfume—she wore enough of it. But what kind did she wear?

Or nail polish. I invented an excuse to sit beside her and notice the shade of red.

What magazines did Helen read? What music did she like? For several days I surreptitiously studied this person I'd been avoiding—discovering in the process a delightful girl who fed stray cats behind the gym and wrote to a pen pal in Australia.

I gained more than a new friend when I drew Helen's name for the party. I gained insight into my reluctance to go down those unfamiliar roads.

People I think I won't like. Skills I won't attempt. Jobs I don't want to undertake.

It isn't dislike. It's lack of faith. Shrinking from the untried because it can't be as good as the known. Failing, from lack of trust, to step into all that God has for me.

*FATHER, give me a pioneer's zest for the untrod road ahead.*

24 *Fog*

*He bowed the heavens, and came down.*
2 SAMUEL 22:10

*F*orty minutes was the scheduled flying time of our flight from Austria to Frankfurt, Germany, where we were to connect with the plane that would take us home to the States for the Christmas holidays. But we'd been in the air an hour now....

Still the plane flew on in the clear blue sky. At last the pilot's voice came on. Of the German words

I caught only *Nebel,* fog. Our seat mate translated for us: visibility in Frankfurt was under 400 meters; the flight was being diverted to Stuttgart from where buses would transport us the rest of the distance to the Frankfurt Airport.

Fog? I looked out my window at the wings of the plane glinting in the sun. Far below us, it was true, was a floor of clouds, almost too bright to look at in the dazzling light.

As we descended through those clouds over Stuttgart, the world outside the window turned gray and raindrops streaked the glass. Once on the ground we were taken by motor coach from Stuttgart to Frankfurt, four hours in the driving rain on a crowded Autobahn. Near Frankfurt the fog thickened. Traffic slowed and snarled.

But this was the route that was taking us to those we love. And I thought, as the bus crawled forward, of the route God took for love of us. Of the One who left the realm of endless day to plunge into the storms of human life, for me.

*Thank You, JESUS, for leaving heaven … for becoming our Companion on the roads we don't want to take.*

# 25 *Bad News*

*Even the darkness is not dark to thee.*

PSALM 139:12

$I$ went outside, after the bad news came, and took my usual path through the woods. Not headed anywhere: too stunned to pray or even to cry. Someone dear to me had died, needlessly, senselessly, and the shock was like a physical blow.

Before, in times of great stress, the woods had spoken to me of a world of beauty and serenity, far removed from the ugliness we men create. That morning no such comfort came.

On the contrary, the peace of the woods seemed an affront to the cruel realities of life. The fluttering leaves, the silly chirping birds were irrelevant to human suffering. I glanced up through the branches at the blue, uncaring sky—and stopped short.

Above my head the trunk of a tree was split in two. One of the halves ended in a jagged stump, perhaps the result of a long-ago lightning strike, while new branches from the surviving half filled in the empty space.

Slowly I walked on. A few yards farther the heart of a chestnut oak was eaten away with disease, a thin outer layer soaring skyward around a hollow core. Here insects had left a gall wound, there a branch was missing. Everywhere I looked were signs of trauma and loss.

But ... all these were living trees—drawing life from the sun, giving it back as food, oxygen, shelter.

It was far from the time when my own wound would grow a protective shell. Farther still till I could turn my healing into help for others. But what I'd seen that morning was sorrow and joy, not as opposites, but as the seamless fabric of life itself.

*FATHER, help me to see the dark threads too as part of Your design.*

*Humility:*

## Taking the Low Road

# 26 Traveling Companion: NAAMAN
## ... who found the humble path

*Naaman ... was a great man.*
2 KINGS 5:1

*T*he man who walks beside us now—or gallops past us in his chariot, as we first meet him—is not a Jew at all but a Syrian, a member of the warlike nation to the north of Israel. Larger, wealthier, Syria looked in contempt on its poor neighbor to the south, and raided and plundered Israel at will.

To Naaman God had an all-important lesson to teach—one as needed today as in the ninth century B.C. For there is one primary roadblock to every spiritual journey in every age.

Pride.

Naaman, it is true, had plenty to be proud about. General of Syria's army, he was "a mighty man of valor" who had won his nation's independence from the great Assyrian Empire. His name literally meant "Delight."

And then … Naaman contracted leprosy.

When that first telltale white spot appeared on General Naaman's body, he was terrified. And terror changed him from a haughty, self-satisfied person to a humble and modest one. Right?

Not at all. Problems do not in themselves make us humble.

Naaman doubtless spent a fortune making the rounds of local miracle workers, paying inflated prices for amulets of locusts' eggs and foxes' teeth.

Nothing helped. The hideous pale patches spread and multiplied. Naaman the Delight of his people became Naaman the Leper. In the normal course of events he would soon replace his linen robes with the sackcloth of mourning, and disappear into one of the outcast colonies that haunted the Damascus city dumps.

And now the God of Israel moves into the story with the first lesson in humility.

## 1. Naaman must accept help from "beneath"

Naaman is used to moving in the best circles. Kings, high priests—"when you need help, go to the top." Meanwhile, beneath Naaman's very nose is a little slave girl, captured in some Syrian raid on an Israeli village. The little captive tells her mistress, Naaman's wife, about a prophet in her own land of

Israel who has a gift of healing.

There are four reasons why the great general would ordinarily pay no attention to her: She's a slave, an Israelite, a female, a child—all, in his eyes, "inferior." How often do we miss a truth of God because it doesn't come in a social or cultural form acceptable to us? But Naaman is grasping at straws.

## 2. He must recognize his poverty

Naaman is desperate enough to follow the advice of a slave girl, but he's still operating through channels. From the king of Syria he secures a letter of recommendation to the king of Israel. Furthermore, he knows the power of money. To pave his way, he takes with him gold, silver, embroidered robes—$100,000 worth of gifts.

But in Israel he discovers that his connections and his cash count for nothing. The king reads the letter and tears his clothes in distress: *He* can't heal leprosy! And the prophet, when Naaman finally realizes he's not to be found in the palace and seeks him out in his humble home, will have none of Naaman's money.

Status and wealth—they ought to help on our journey, but all too often they hinder. As long as Naaman is counting on his high-placed friends and his camel-loads of gifts, he is not seeking God.

### 3. He must give up his own scenario

Naaman gallops up to the prophet's door in his splendid chariot with his retinue of mounted attendants, making considerable clatter. He pictures in his mind how it will be. The healer will come out (a little awed—he doesn't often get a client like *me* in this one-horse burg!) and begin an elaborate sequence of chants and incantations.

How often we try to dictate *how* God's help is to come! But the prophet does none of the things Naaman expects. He doesn't even put in an appearance. To the proud Syrian general he sends out a message: "Go and wash in the Jordan seven times."

Naaman storms away. A nobody prophet from a nothing nation first slights him, then sends him off on an idiot's errand. If it's a river that's needed, Syria has better ones than this little trickle of a Jordan! But it is his crucial third lesson in humility: If Naaman had been able to specify the means of his healing, he and not God would have remained in charge.

### 4. He must stop trying to earn God's gift

Once more it is a mere servant, one of his own attendants, who speaks the word of God to Naaman: "If the prophet had commanded you to do some great thing, would you not have done it?"

Of course he would! So would we! Some great

act of devotion, some noble sacrifice—some contribution, in other words, on our part, to the benefit we hope to receive. To receive it wholly as a gift, to take it without an ounce of merit on our side, to be totally in God's debt—this is what our pride finds hardest. Just ... dunk up and down in a river? It sounds too easy. Surely He requires more of us?

But at last proud Naaman steps into the muddy Jordan.

Incredulous, unable at first to grasp what is happening, Naaman watches his putrefying skin become "like the flesh of a little child."

Naaman hurries back to the prophet's house. This time he dismounts from his chariot and stands humbly before the door, and this time the man of God comes out to greet him ... as God greets us, too, when we climb off our high horse.

Out of gratitude now, no longer trying to buy God's favor, Naaman again attempts to present his costly gifts. But the prophet will not accept them even now, for the Syrian has a last lesson to learn. God, not man, is the giver—last as well as first. The way we enter on the walk of faith ... by coming with empty hands to His mercy ... is the way we continue in it: asking in order to receive.

*LORD, I am grateful that I never cease to need: need sets me on the low road to Your high calling.*

# 27 Riches

*A man's life does not consist in the*
*abundance of his possessions.*
LUKE 12:15

*I*t's Bulk Trash pickup on our street tomorrow, and all week beside the road the piles of cast-offs have been growing. Discarded storm windows, an old TV, a broken tricycle.

Driving past these heaps of discards I've been seeing another street—the road past our house in Uganda—and a man literally leaping for joy as he walked ...

The house we'd rented in that central African nation was in a neighborhood of mud-walled homes strung along a red-earth track. There was no trash pickup there; nobody threw things out. Our house, in fact, had the only trash can along that road: a small lidless barrel that we would take at infrequent intervals to a public dump.

One morning I answered a knock to find a neighbor standing at the door. In his hands was an orange-soda bottle I had put in the barrel the evening before.

"Pardon for this disturbance," he began in the formal school-learned English of Uganda, "but as I passed your house my eyes beheld this." He held up the empty bottle. "I have asked of myself," he stammered on, "is it that you have no further plan for it? I am not a thief," he added hastily. "It is only that finding it here in this barrel ..."

I was the one now to stammer for words. "Of course ... take it," I said. "I'm just sorry I didn't—I should have offered it in a more ..."

But at the words "take it," he had headed off up the road. The last I saw of him he was running, leaping, all but dancing along that dirt track in the exhilaration of sudden wealth.

I've been thinking about that man as the trash piles grow along our street. Ours has been called the throw-away society—stripping the forests, polluting the seas, despoiling the earth. If we made do with less, I've been asking myself, might we too dance with the joy of gratitude?

*FATHER, we would not be rich in things, therefore poor in soul.*

# 28 *Laurel*

*The very stone which the builders
rejected has become the head of the
corner.*

LUKE 20:17

*I*n the Shawangunk Mountains, seventy-five miles
from our home, is an unspoiled lake where I go
when my spirit needs recharging. Shaded and
inviting in summer, scarlet and gold in fall, pristine
and silent in winter, Mohonk is special in all
seasons. But the most spectacular time of year there
is May, when the mountain laurel turns whole
hillsides pink and white. People from all over the
world come then to gaze at nature in her most
blithesome mood.

Laurel wasn't always so appreciated. In fact, it
was the presence of this "weed shrub" that, in 1869,
made it possible for two Quaker brothers to
purchase the lake and the land around it. Albert and
Alfred Smiley had a conviction that scenic natural
areas ought to be preserved for coming generations
to enjoy. Land costs money, however, and the

Smileys didn't have a lot of it. It didn't take much money, though, to buy land "infested" with laurel. "It never grows big enough for firewood," one local farmer complained as he signed the sale papers. "And cattle won't eat the good-for-nothing stuff."

Good for nothing ... except refreshment of the body and renewal of the heart and mind.

> *What humble gift of Yours have I failed to value? LORD, show me the laurel in my life today.*

## 29    *Communion*

*Consider the lilies of the field.*
MATTHEW 6:28

*T*he elderly Japanese gardener bent so close that his wisp of a beard stroked the needles of the tiny tree. The 200-year-old pine was only 18 inches high, an exquisite specimen of the art of bonsai.

The gardener moved on to a miniature maple, again lowering his head in what seemed an intimate communion. There was much more to see in San Francisco's Golden Gate Park, but I couldn't tear my eyes from this relationship between a man and the living things in his care.

Next he stopped over a small sturdy oak, then a 2-foot-high cedar, product of nearly 300 years of devoted care. What empathy with roots and soil, sap and bark, generation after generation, had gone into the nurturing of these trees!

I waited till the gardener straightened again. "Excuse me, sir," I said. "Would you tell me—when you bend down ... are you speaking to the trees?"

The old man turned to me a face seemingly as full of age and wisdom as the trees themselves. "No," he answered. "I do not speak to the trees. I listen to them."

*LORD, teach us the language of Your creation.*

## 30    *Traveler's Aid ... Practicing Humility*

> *Clothe yourselves, all of you, with*
> *humility ... for God opposes the proud,*
> *but gives grace to the humble.*
> 1 PETER 5:5

*H*ow do we put on this pilgrim garb of humility?
Today we begin a week-long exercise in this most
essential and elusive of virtues, using as our guide
Philippians 2:6–8. Here Paul describes Jesus:

> *who, though he was in the form of God ...*
> *emptied himself, taking the form of a*
> *servant, being born in the likeness of men.*
> *And being found in human form he*
> *humbled himself and became obedient unto*
> *death, even death on a cross.*

To start, picture yourself standing next to One
"in the form of God." Your own status, possessions,
skills, education—how inconsequential they seem
next to Him! Now apply what follows to yourself, a
phrase each day.

Sunday ... he *emptied himself,* in the King James wording: *made himself of no reputation* ... How important to you is the way you appear to others? How much care will you take today dressing for church? Would you risk the community's high opinion to champion an unpopular cause? How much energy do you expend making sure you are not misunderstood or misjudged? Jesus' answer was to "empty himself" of all such concerns.

Monday ... *taking the form of a servant* ... Whether your job is in an office, a factory, a schoolroom, or at home—what is your purpose in working? Is it essentially to better yourself, to have more, to reach the top? Or do you measure success in terms of service to others? Is there some task you can perform today for which you will receive no credit—which only you and God will know about?

Tuesday ... *being born in the likeness of men* ... God has many servants in the universe; Jesus could have done service as an archangel. But He chose instead to take human form, and that meant all the restrictions of our flesh and blood—physical drives, weariness, pain, separation, limitations on our power to act and know—even limits on our ability to accomplish things for God. How will you react today to the frustrations of your mortality?

Wednesday ... *And being found in human form, he humbled himself* ... Even as a human being, Jesus could have had pomp and honor. Instead He became a manual laborer in an insignificant town in a backwater province of a conquered country. How do you evaluate the importance of people around you? Does the kind of work they do, their social standing, affect the way you look at them? Try to see the people you meet today through Jesus' eyes.

Thursday ... *and became obedient* ... Obedience is a word out of favor today. We no longer obey kings or priests—and often not parents, teachers or policemen either. Yet emancipated though we imagine ourselves, we are all, in fact, obedient every day of our lives. If not to higher authorities, then to lower, less easily recognized ones: our own wants and urges, an ad campaign, the opinions of a peer group. Before you make decisions today, ask Jesus what voice you are obeying.

Friday ... *unto death* ... The ultimate self-relinquishment is death. This is why we struggle so fiercely against anything that threatens our self-esteem. The whole bundle of self-awareness that we call ego cries out that survival is at stake. Every Friday is a little commemoration of Good Friday when Jesus accepted death on our behalf. Ask Him what attitudes, habits, and prejudices can begin to die in you.

Saturday ... *even death on a cross* ... There are many ways to die. There is the hero's death on a battlefield; there is death eased by the skill of doctors, comforted by the closeness of loved ones. Jesus' death was neither glorious nor easy. If life does not treat you as well today as you feel you deserve, if friends are not as loyal as you would wish, can you borrow for a while His acceptance and benediction?

If you can—if you can learn humility from Christ—you can also begin to share in His glory. Every Sunday is a little celebration of the Easter victory. "Therefore," Paul joyously concludes his portrait, "God has highly exalted him and bestowed on him the name which is above every name" (Phil. 2:9).

The resurrection promise is not to Jesus only, but to all who follow the lowly path He pioneered. "For every one who exalts himself will be humbled, and he who humbles himself will be exalted" (Luke 14:11).

*Perseverance:*

# When Progress Seems Slow

## 31 *Traveling Companion:* MOSES *... who learned the value of a detour*

*Then we turned and journeyed into*
*the wilderness ... as the LORD told me.*
DEUTERONOMY 2:1

*M*oses! Sublime, awesome—can you and I really walk beside this greatest figure of the Old Testament? Won't we be like pygmies trying to keep pace with a giant?

Actually, our very hesitance to join such grand company can be our first step together. "Moses was very meek, more than all men that were on the face of the earth," and when this humble and unassuming person heard that God had tapped him for a supremely important journey, his response was exactly what ours is:

"Who am I that I should go to Pharaoh?"

Of course God knew all about Moses' poor self-image and his speech impediment—as He knows each of our shortcomings—and so He heaped encouragements and reassurances on him, as He does on us. God himself would go with him, He would deal with the opposition, He would work signs and miracles on Moses' behalf. And Moses, after hearing it all, answers:

"Please, Lord, send someone else."

This is the kind of man I can walk with. The journey into freedom—this is the central theme of Moses' life. Whether our slavery is literal, as it was for the Hebrews in Egypt and blacks in America, or figurative; whether it's physical—to drugs or cigarettes or chocolate brownies—or emotional, we can follow the road that Moses pioneered. But … what a strange road, filled with false starts and seeming dead-ends.

*Why detours?*

Some years ago when my own bondage took the form of an incapacitating depression, friends kept urging me to "snap out of it." "Look on the bright side!" they'd say. "Stop being negative."

Like saying to an alcoholic: stop drinking! Or to the chronic worrier: be confident! Go from wherever your Egypt is, directly into the Promised Land!

Over and over I tried to follow such well-meaning advice. I wore a perpetual smile, I made lists of things I had to be thankful for, I denied the misery that engulfed me—to no avail.

For me the true route out of depression was a circuitous one, involving repeated journeys into the wilderness of memory, a confronting of my own "wild beasts."

It often seemed that I was making no progress—was even going backward, toward the very darkness I wished to escape. And yet this painful and seemingly indirect approach proved the path to lasting freedom.

So it was for the Hebrew slaves of Pharaoh, and so it may be for your own form of bondage. Instead of chafing at the detours in your path, ask yourself this month how God is using them.

## 1. To enlarge our vision

Moses was an idealistic young man. He hated bullies, whether it was an Egyptian brutalizing a Hebrew, or a group of men shoving a woman away from a watering trough. Perhaps he dreamed of using his influence as the foster son of an Egyptian princess to outlaw the use of the whip, or shorten the working day.

Instead, with one hasty ill-timed deed he found himself, at age forty, exiled from the people he meant to help. To him it must have seemed as if he'd thrown away his chances, given up whatever leverage he had at court, to come to some godforsaken wilderness and herd a bunch of silly sheep.

How could Moses know that the trouble with his original dream was not that it was not big enough? That he was called not to improve working conditions in a particular slave labor camp, but to lead an entire people away from slavery forever?

## 2. To give us specific training

God knew that the skills of the desert sheepherder ... knowledge of the weather ... the secret of water trapped in limestone ... the location of oases ... were precisely the know-how Moses would need to lead not sheep but men, women and children through the wilderness. What must have seemed to Moses years of tedious routine—wasted years in terms of his youthful dream—were in God's all-seeing economy the perfect preparation for the work that lay ahead.

## 3. To temper our faith

After harrowing confrontations with Pharaoh, Moses led his people out of Egypt. But what a strange roundabout route they traveled! Their destination—our destination—was the Promised Land, where the good things of God were waiting. But "God did not lead them by way of the land of the Philistines, although that was near."

The "way of the Philistines" was the coastal highway patrolled by Pharaoh's army. It was the shortest way to the Promised Land, but one where the escaping slaves might face a battle around any bend ... before they were toughened and disciplined by the wilderness experience.

Why aren't our lives a straight line? Why does a medical student have to interrupt his education to work as a taxi driver? Why does an artist starve for years before he sells a painting? Why doesn't God make His guidance clearer? Probably because the success that comes too easily, the faith that encounters no obstacles, is the one that crumbles with the first opposition.

### 4. To give us another chance

"Turn tomorrow and set out for the wilderness." Finally came the longest detour of all, the most heartbreaking. On the very threshold of the Promised Land, within sight of all that God had for them, God's people panicked. His miracles of provision and protection forgotten, they clamored only to return to the slavery and safety of Egypt.

A year and a half in the wilderness had not sufficed for basic training: this detour was to last forty years and see the deaths of all those whose faith had wavered.

It was a devastating blow to Moses, and yet it corresponds to our own experience. We cannot receive the freedom God holds out to us while any part of us longs to return to Egypt ... to the old dependent, enslaving patterns. Only "the children"—the new life in us—the qualities nurtured and strengthened on the desert marches, will prove fit for life in His kingdom.

*LORD, let me learn the lessons of the wilderness through which I am passing ... so that I do not have to retrace these steps again!*

## 32    *Waiting*

*FATHER, I thank thee that thou hast heard me.*
JOHN 11:41

*I*'d gone on the weekend retreat with a question about unanswered prayer. Holy Cross Monastery is a beautiful set-apart space on the banks of the Hudson River eighty miles north of New York City, where I'd taken questions in the past. Somewhere in that prayerful place, perhaps during a chapel service, perhaps in the course of a talk by the retreat leader, answers had come.

The concern I brought to this particular weekend was a long-standing one: the need of someone God loved very much to begin loving himself. Many people for many years had prayed for this to happen. The question I'd brought to this retreat was "Why?" Why is there no change? Why is persevering prayer so unavailing?

An answer came, too, as I expected it would. It didn't come in the chapel, though, or the lecture room. It came as I walked along the narrow shale beach at the edge of the river. The Hudson is wide and calm there: across the water rises the classical facade of the Vanderbilt mansion at Hyde Park.

A family of ducks was feeding near the shore. As I stopped to watch them, a giant oil tanker passed. Huge and silent, it filled the whole horizon. Then, moving swiftly downriver, it grew smaller, leaving the water's broad surface as undisturbed as though no ship had gone by. I strolled on downstream, watching the tanker disappear around the bend.

The noise came from behind me—a roar like an approaching freight train. I whirled around to see two-foot waves rushing toward me across the water. Curling, cresting, crashing in white foam around my feet. Where had they come from! What had suddenly roiled the water on this windless morning?

Of course: the tanker! The ship I'd almost forgotten, now out of sight.

I had wet shoes as I started back up the path to the monastery, but I had an answer, too, which satisfies me as I wait for results of so much prayer. Persevering effort is not unavailing. Our pleas are registered in heaven and God's redeeming power is in motion. The effect has simply not reached the surface of things where our human eyes are fixed.

*LORD, give me the grace to walk by faith, not by seeing.*

## 33    Repentance

*A time to break down, and a time to build up....*
ECCLESIASTES 3:3

*B*ecause older women in my family have endured the stooped backs and broken bones of osteoporosis, I decided recently to do some reading on prevention. In the library I pored over charts and chemical analyses, but it was a sentence in one of the books that struck me most: "Like all living tissue, bone is constantly being broken down and re-formed."

The words seemed to apply not only to our bodies but to the perpetual Christian emphasis on brokenness. Repent! Confess! Acknowledge your sinfulness! I grow tired of this continual retracing of steps, impatient for the beckoning road ahead.

But it was the word *living* that leaped out at me: It's living tissue that is continually torn down and rebuilt. As long as my relationship to God is alive, this biological fact seems to suggest, the tearing-down process will be part of it. The confession of sin, the admission of guilt, will go hand in hand with renewal. Whether it's laying down ownership of a project so that others can run with it or taking our controlling fingers out of our children's lives, there can be no growth without pruning, no rebirth without death.

The medical name for this continuous cycle of breakdown and reformation, my reading informed me, is "bone-remodeling."

Soul-remodeling—isn't that another name for this spiritual pilgrimage? Repentance, forgiveness, new life. An essential sequence, not just now and then, but at every stage of our journey.

> *Thank You, LORD, for the backward steps*
> *that enable us to move forward.*

## 34 *Wilderness*

*O that my ways may be steadfast.*
PSALM 119:5

$M$y husband and I have a system for exploring
new hiking trails. One of us will start at the
beginning while the other takes the car to the
opposite end and hikes back the other way toward a
rendezvous somewhere deep in the hills or the
forest.

We've seen some of America's loveliest
wilderness this way, and added something special to
our relationship. All along the path I'll find myself
saving up small adventures to share when we meet.
Questions, too, about unfamiliar sights and sounds.

As our steps draw nearer, my anticipation
mounts. Around any curve now he may appear ...
perhaps beyond that hemlock grove, or over that
rise. When the trail's been long and I'm growing
tired, expectation keeps me pressing forward. Soon,
very soon, I'll see him coming. Any minute now ...

*When the road is long, FATHER, and the
journeying hard, this knowledge helps me*

*persevere: Though I don't yet see You, I*
*know that every step brings closer the*
*moment of Your appearing.*

## 35       *Oil Strike*

*For my thoughts are not your thoughts,*
*neither are your ways my ways, says the*
LORD.

ISAIAH 55:8

*I*t was on a trip to Texas that I heard a story which
suggests the kind of perseverance God requires.
Steadfastness that sticks to our purpose through
trials and disappointment—but not so obsessively
that we leave no room for grace....

John and I had attended church in the town of
Kilgore. Chatting with old-timers on the lawn
afterward, we heard the story of Doc Lloyd and Dad
Joiner, back in the days when this energetic city was
a country crossroads.

Doc Lloyd was an independent oil geologist
from Fort Worth who'd often worked with seventy-

year-old wildcatter C. M. Joiner. In 1929, the two men drew the scorn of the close-knit fraternity of Texas oilmen by maintaining that there was oil in the Kilgore area—specifically, beneath the farm of a woman named Daisy Bradford. Published analyses pointed to a score of reasons why there couldn't be oil, not anywhere around there. Just because Doc had brought in three successful wells for Dad in the past, did that make him smarter than the big-company experts?

Lloyd and Joiner drilled on Daisy's land anyhow. And failed, just as everyone said they would. They drilled again. And failed again. Their money was gone but Daisy gave them an extension on their drilling option. Why not? The land wasn't good for anything but cattle ranching, and not much good for that.

For the third time Doc and Dad hoisted their huge derrick onto a skid and hauled it over the uneven ground toward yet another drilling site. Halfway there, however, the well-worn skid itself broke down. At this point less determined men would have quit. But quitting wasn't Doc's and Dad's way. If they couldn't get the derrick to the place they intended to drill, the two men decided they'd drill where they were.

They found oil.

Not just a single well: Lloyd and Joiner had stumbled on the richest oil field ever found in the

United States. Over four and a half billion barrels have been recovered to date, and the wells are still pumping.

*LORD, give me courage to keep going ...*
*and grace to look to You when I can't. It*
*may be that Your richest gift lies right*
*beneath my feet.*

*Servanthood:*

## Laying Down Our Own Itinerary

## 36 Traveling Companion: ABRAHAM'S SERVANT ... who journeyed for another

*And Abraham said to his servant ...*
*"Go to my country and to my kindred,*
*and take a wife for my son Isaac."*
GENESIS 24:2, 4

*I*t's exhilarating to travel with famous men of faith—with Moses, Abraham, Elisha. The man with whom we are journeying now, however, is not even given a name. He had one, of course, ancestors, hopes and fears, most likely a wife and children. But these details about him—if they were known to those who first recounted his story around the tribal campfires—were not considered worth preserving when the time came to commit the history of Israel to paper. He thus becomes a fit companion for all of us "nobodies" on this path of faith.

But though his name was not recorded, his contribution *was*—set down for all time in sacred

Scripture. Without this anonymous individual, in fact, the Bible would close with the book of Genesis. On the faithful carrying-out of the task assigned him hinged the future of God's chosen people.

He could not have foreseen the importance of his assignment, any more than you and I can see the link between our daily duties and God's all-inclusive plan. But no chain can spare any link—not my contribution, not yours. Only God sees the grand design from beginning to end; our responsibility is to discharge our particular assignment. To discover, in other words,

*The serenity of servanthood.*

Throughout the Old Testament great value is placed on faithful servants. It isn't until the New Testament, however—when God himself comes to earth as a servant (Phil. 2:7)—that servanthood begins to be seen not just as *an* acceptable role but as *the* God-given calling of all believers.

It's a hard concept for us today. The whole tradition of the personal servant seems to belong to a happily outgrown past. Most of us are neither servants nor masters—while for most of human history every man, woman, and child was one or the other.

Where shall we go in this servantless age to find a role model for our own servanthood? What are the standards by which a servant is judged?

There is only one: his master's evaluation. Anyone else's opinion of a servant's performance— even his own—simply doesn't matter. "Who are you to pass judgement on the servant of another?" demands St. Paul. "It is before his own master that he stands or falls" (Rom. 14:4). When we become servants of God we cease having to care about satisfying anybody else.

Abraham's servant is our model. How do we know he was a good one? Because Abraham thought so: He "had charge of all that he had." Let's watch the way this good servant carried out his task.

## 1. He got his orders clear

So often we catch a glimpse of the divine mission and dash off without establishing the limits of our assignment. The experienced servant of Abraham, before setting out on *his* journey, made sure he understood what he was *not* to do.

Limited tasks can be the hardest of all. To speak a word, to write a letter—and then *take our hands off*—this is the heart of servanthood: "I planted, Apollos watered," wrote Paul, "but God gave the growth…. What then is Apollos? What is Paul? Servants…" (1 Cor. 3:6, 5).

## 2. He prayed as he obeyed

External obedience, the perfunctory carrying-out of a command, could be compelled by an all-powerful human master. And it can be compelled in us by a false image of a harsh and punitive God.

Our companion today did not give grudging service based on fear. He was Abraham's man—heart and soul, as well as body— praying for the success of his journey as he covered the miles.

### 3. He knew how to wait

Having placed in God's hands the choice of a wife for his master's son, "the man gazed at her in silence to learn whether the Lord had prospered his journey or not." At the sight of Rebekah, everything in the servant must have cried out, "This is the one!" Young, beautiful, gracious, kind—surely his mission was a brilliant success! And he had ten camel loads of gifts with which to influence events.

But as a servant he had learned to wait the pleasure of another. Only after the sign from God was given did he draw some jewelry from his saddlebags.

### 4. He put his master's interests first

After the long trek from Canaan to Mesopotamia, Abraham's servant was dusty, tired, and above all hungry. But his assignment from Abraham was a trust that came ahead of everything. "Then food was set before him to eat; but he said, 'I will not eat until I have told my errand.' "

Rebekah and her family agree to the betrothal,

but want her to remain at home "at least ten days."
Abraham's servant is not a young man. Ten days to
rest and enjoy fabled Near Eastern hospitality before
setting out once more on a rigorous journey is
surely not self-indulgent.

"But he said to them, 'Do not delay me, since
the Lord has prospered my way; let me go that I
may go to my master.' ... Then Rebekah and her
maids arose, and rode upon the camels and
followed the man."

That I may go to my master ...

*LORD, help me to know that servanthood is
the royal road to Your kingdom.*

# 37 *Robbers*

*The thief comes only to steal and kill
and destroy.*

JOHN 10:10

*I*t's a parable of the world in balance. Deep within
the scarlet flower of the trumpet vine lies the nectar
on which the humming bird depends to fuel his
darting flight. And as the bird probes inside the
trumpet its feathers collect pollen which it carries to
neighboring vines. The stationary plant reproduces
itself, the energy-hungry bird is fed.

On the slopes of the Andes Mountains, however,
a different kind of bird is at work. Called a flower
piercer, this species has learned to circumvent
nature's design. Instead of entering the mouth of
the trumpet, as the flower's glory of color beckons it
to do, the flower piercer stabs a hole from outside
directly into the nectar chamber ... gorging itself on
the sweet fluid, giving nothing in return.

No harm seems to be done in the teeming life
of the Andean jungle. Humming birds outnumber
flower piercers. But a nightmare vision haunts me.

What if the flower piercers somehow became numerous enough and clever enough to eliminate the hummers? What if the robber-birds had it all their own way?

The vines would die out, of course ... and so would the flower piercers. In my nightmare the earth has become that glorious vine, mankind that short-sighted bird.

> *LORD, teach us to obey the laws Love has written into the universe.*

## 38    *Self-Portrait*

> *It is required of stewards that they be found trustworthy.*
> 1 CORINTHIANS 4:2

*T*hey appeared in the early sixties, those first photographs from space. They changed forever the way we see the earth.

For the first time we beheld our planet whole: a blue-and-white jewel set in the blackness of the

118

universe, lovely beyond imagining.

Fragile beyond imagining, too—a shimmering dot in the yawning immensity of space. No longer the enormous earth men had struggled to explore and conquer: a mountain here, an ocean there, elsewhere a desert or a forest. Our portrait from space showed us a unity, a little ball, bound together and interconnected in every part.

But the revelation wasn't new, not really. That view of ourselves from beyond ourselves is God's view—the picture the Bible painted long before the camera caught it.

God created the earth whole. He made it beautiful. He created Adam, "Earthman," to tend it in His name.

Over our kitchen table my husband and I have a magnetic board where we post reminders to prayer. There since the 1960s, among pictures of family and friends, we've kept a photograph of our planet, inspiring us to ask each day:

*LORD, make us faithful stewards of the earth.*

# 39     *Expectations*

*And I will make all my mountains a
way, and my highways shall be raised
up.*

ISAIAH 49:11

*T*he monastery was erected on its hill above the
Hudson River in 1902: a three-story red brick, dutch
colonial structure. But the interesting thing to me
about the building is the way it's oriented. The main
entrance faces the river, the dock and the long
driveway up from the water by which, it was
assumed, people would arrive.

Amazing to recall that as late as the early years of
this century, the river was still the chief
thoroughfare of the area. Dirt roads, dusty or
muddy, depending on the season, served local
farmers, and there was passenger train service on
the opposite shore. But on this side of the river, fast
modern steamboats provided by far the most
dependable transportation.

Automobiles? They were too new, too few, too
experimental for most people to glimpse their
potential.

Those scheduled daily steamboat runs must have seemed as dependable as the tides that sweep up the river from the sea. The monastery's designers never questioned positioning the front door facing the boat landing. But that driveway up from the river's edge was never actually built. Automobile highway construction was begun about the time the monastery opened, and for nine decades people have been coming in ... through the back door.

It makes me think of our assumptions about God, and the avenues we expect Him to use to achieve His purposes. How often we limit Him with our preconceived ideas of the way He's going to enter our lives. How often He surprises us by turning up where we least expect Him.

*How wonderful, LORD, to serve a Master of infinite invention!*

*Coping:*

# When the
# Road Is Rough

# 40 Traveling Companion: JOSEPH ... who traveled light

*[His brothers] sold him to the Ishmaelites ... and they took Joseph to Egypt.*
GENESIS 37:28

*T*hinking of our lives as a journey, we focus naturally on goals—where we hope to arrive, how far we must travel to get there.

But there's another kind of journey each of us must take—sometimes over and over: the trip to the place we never wanted to go. Maybe it's early widowhood ... a crushing financial reverse ... just the process of aging. Perhaps it's a literal trip like the one neighbors of ours took recently to a midwestern mental hospital where their college sophomore daughter had just been committed.

Whatever the crisis, there you are, on this unwelcome journey, surrounded by people and circumstances far from your own choosing, expected to function at unfamiliar tasks when your whole being cries out to return to the way things used to be.

Joseph is good company on such a trek. What must his thoughts have been on that bitter march through the Negev, the hottest part of the Syria-Egypt caravan route, hands bound behind him, throat thick with the dust raised by hundreds of camels. Every painful step was taking him farther from the home where everything had been going his way.

Favorite child of a wealthy father, he'd been exempt from the physical labor expected of his brothers. Older translators had it that his father gave him a coat "of many colors," but a more accurate rendition is "a long coat with sleeves"—the coat of a gentleman who does not need to work with his hands.

From a position of privilege he'd plunged to the status of a slave—a nonperson—hauled against his will into a menacing land.

*Unneeded luggage: "It's not fair!"*

It would be understandable if Joseph—if we—gave in to self-pity. Especially as it all came about while he was doing what his father told him to! Disaster had struck through no fault of his own, and the sense of injustice could have become the heaviest burden on this unwelcome march.

125

Nor did the unfairness stop there. When, making the best of a negative situation, Joseph managed through hard work to carve out a respected position for himself as a slave, a second undeserved blow fell. Falsely accused of a shameful crime, he was removed from his post and thrown into prison.

It makes me think of a former schoolmate left at her husband's death with two young children and mammoth hospital bills. By going without new clothes or vacations or bicycles for the children, she managed to build up a small greeting-card business—only to have her partner make off with the money, leaving her once again saddled with debts.

*Unneeded luggage: "What's the use in trying?"*

The objective problems my friend faced at this point were daunting enough. What made them overwhelming was the load of emotions she had to carry along with them. "What's the use?" became her answer to all offers of assistance.

Repeated blows often lead to this sense of hopelessness. For Joseph they did not. We know this because of the way he acted. Despair paralyzes, but Joseph threw himself with immense energy into each new situation, however distasteful. In prison he was soon singled out, as he had been in slavery, as a natural administrator.

Obviously Joseph "traveled light"; he didn't drag

with him a burden of destructive feelings. What was his secret?

The Lord was with Joseph.

Joseph knew that there is no land so far, no dungeon so deep that God does not precede us there. Cut off from friends and family, locked behind bars, he is not cut off from God.

*Unneeded luggage: "They did me in."*

There was a last piece of baggage—the bulkiest, most encumbering of all—which Joseph might well have lugged to his grave.

Resentment.

Almost any misfortune seems bearable except the one brought on by the malice of other people. Illness, accident, earthquake, these may tempt us to self-pity, even despair—but betrayal invites the bitterness that corrodes the soul.

My school friend, so courageous and resourceful in coping with debt brought about by her husband's cancer, was utterly unable to deal with the same thing caused by the dishonesty of her partner.

Joseph's problems too were the result of human ill will: his brothers' jealousy, a frame-up by his master's wife. And still another example of human fallibility awaited him: A fellow prisoner to whom he had rendered a service was released ... and promptly forgot about the good word he was to put in on Joseph's behalf. It slipped his mind for two whole years—years that Joseph, down in the dungeon, might have spent brooding on the faithlessness of human nature.

But human nature was not where his attention was fixed. His eyes were on God. Not: "What have people done?" But: "What is God doing?"

### Setting down that unwanted luggage

*Forgiveness* is the theological name for what we do when we put down our suitcasefull of wrongs and injuries. People who worked with concentration camp survivors after World War II reported that those who were able to forgive were able to resume their life journeys; those who held on to their resentments were condemned to walk forever the treadmill of the past.

How can we forgive the monstrous and terrible? Joseph shows us. The way is not to deny the awfulness of what has happened—the dishonest partner, the scheming brothers, the ovens of Auschwitz. Glossing over the truth only separates us from Truth himself. "*You meant evil against me,*" Joseph tells his brothers. To call their action anything but evil would be a lie. But that's not the whole story—or even the important part. "You meant evil, *but God meant it for good.*"

Try substituting the name of whoever is

wronging you in place of Joseph's brothers: "(Fred,) (The management,) (The burglar who broke into my home) mean evil against me, but God means it for good."

Joseph lived to see with his own eyes the good that God intended. Whether you and I do or not, we can echo his words to his brothers, along whatever dark path our journey leads: "It was not you who sent me here, but God" (Gen. 45:8).

*LORD, when my route leads into Egypt, it is enough for me that You know why.*

# 41 *Clouds*

*For now we see in a mirror dimly.*
1 CORINTHIANS 13:12

*I*t had been an overcast day, but the forecast was for clearing by midnight. Just in time! In the early-morning hours of August 12 each year, the sky puts on the annual spectacular known as the Perseid meteor shower. That's when the orbiting earth crosses the debris left behind by a long-vanished comet. As specks of this interplanetary matter enter our atmosphere, they burn up, blazing briefly across the night sky as "shooting stars," as many as a hundred an hour.

At 12:30 A.M., armed with a thermos of strong black coffee, John and I drove to the high school playing field, the largest open space around.

Not a star was in sight. At 1:00, still cloudy. One-thirty, 2:00—no change in the leaden skies. At 2:45, a revised weather forecast on the car radio told us what we could see for ourselves: "variable cloudiness and rain the rest of tonight."

Gloomily, we returned home: There would be no Perseid shower this year. After so much coffee, I was a long time falling asleep. And as I lay there, a little parable came. No meteor shower? Of course there was! Miles above us, the celestial fireworks were taking place at this very moment.

It wasn't "the sky" that was gray tonight; it was a local cloud cover affecting a few square miles of the earth's surface. How often, I wondered, have I let my own interior weather condition—some temporary frustration, some passing situation— cloud my vision of what God is doing in His world?

*When I'm tempted to despair, LORD, remind me that a very small cloud can block out a very big heaven.*

## 42      *Bird's Nest*

*The LORD is risen indeed.*
LUKE 24:34

*I*t had been a long trip, leaving home just after
Christmas, getting back a week after Easter. We'd
been in Singapore, on the equator, where there is
no springtime. And now upon returning home
there were no clues to the resurrection season in
our house either.

"It's almost as though Easter never happened
this year," I moped to John as we took soiled
clothing from our suitcases. I was having my usual
case of post-trip letdown. I carried an armload of
clothes to the basement. There was no sense in
getting out the Easter decorations now. "But at
least," I called upstairs, "let's take that dried-out old
Christmas wreath off the door!"

A few moments later John came bounding down
the stairs. "Come with me!" he said. "Out the back
door!"

Silently he led me around to the front of the
house. A small brown finch and her red-headed

mate scolded from a maple as we tiptoed to the front door. Among the browning hemlock twigs of the Christmas wreath a tiny round nest held three speckled eggs.

All three have hatched now: three down-covered chicks many times the size of those tiny eggs. How was so much peeping energy and eagerness ever enclosed in those confining shells? How did a tomb ever contain the Lord of Life himself?

Of course, we haven't been able to use our front door since getting home—and we're getting a little tired of those basement stairs. But that's a small price to pay for the greatest Easter decoration we've ever had.

*LORD, help me to remember that my preparations, my striving, are not what bring renewal ... but Your unconquerable life.*

# 43 *Song Finch*

*In the world you have tribulation; but be of good cheer, I have overcome the world.*

JOHN 16:33

*I*'ve been watching the mother finch who's raising her family on our front door. She has three young ones in her nest—perhaps that's why her flittings and flutterings remind me of myself when our own three were young.

There's a deeper parallel, though. Raising a family, at the outset, probably didn't seem an especially daunting prospect to this drab little bird. She and her handsome mate, after all, had found a nesting site far removed from ugliness and danger. Our unoccupied house seemed to offer a snug private world in which to bring up the children.

The truth about that world turned out to be very different. The isolated haven was revealed—on our return home—to be the front doorway of a very busy household. Unthinkable monsters shared her children's very neighborhood.

As a mother of the Vietnam era, I sympathize with this small, nervous bird. Who had heard, when we built our nest here in the 1950s, of drugs in the quiet suburbs, student strikes in the high school? The birds aren't giving up, of course. Parents don't.

People don't. Whatever the goal, we don't quit when the journey turns out to be longer and harder than we knew.

But the birds are teaching me a secret about keeping on in the face of unexpected hardship. Whenever they can snatch a moment from their anxious labors, the finches sing.

*LORD, give me a song of praise for the rough road ahead.*

# 44 _Landlord_

> _He who dwells in the shelter of the Most_
> _High, who abides in the shadow of the_
> _Almighty, will say to the_ LORD, _"My_
> _refuge and my fortress; my God in_
> _whom I trust."_
>
> PSALM 91:1, 2

_I_'m learning something else as I watch that mother finch—something she's as slow to grasp as I've been. I'm getting a little annoyed, in fact, at the time it's taking her.

Can't the silly bird see that I'm her friend and protector? Her landlord, if it comes to that. That's _my_ door she's squatting on, _my_ front entrance she's taken over. A dozen times a day I have to trudge down to the basement and out the back way. I bang on the window at deliverymen to preserve the sanctity of her home, work with the windows closed lest the sound of my typewriter ruffle her peace of mind.

Her response? To fly away with a squawk every time she catches sight of me.

It's made me wonder about the protection *I* take for granted ... the times God has intervened on my behalf, without my knowing. How often, instead, have I fled His approach, fearful for my comfort, my status quo, my pleasures? How often has the Owner of the place, in spite of my outcries, safeguarded my shelter of twigs and straw? How long has He waited for a word of thanks?

*LORD, thank You.*

*When Our Way Lies
Through Deep Water:*

*Traveling in
Terrifying
Times*

# 45 Traveling Companion: NOAH ... who walked with God

*NOAH was a righteous man, blameless in his generation.*
GENESIS 6:9

*I*f your spiritual journey sets you at odds with the world around you, Noah knew the feeling. He was all alone in his priorities. Noah is thus the perfect travel partner for those times when the path of righteousness seems a lonely and thankless one. What was his secret? How do we go against the crowd? The answer is given in four words:

*Noah walked with God.*

He *walked*. He didn't come running to God when the rain clouds darkened the sky. Daily, hourly, he kept in step, discerning God's presence in small events, so that when the overwhelming event came, he was prepared.

It's a verse that helps me understand something that used to bother me: What about the other people? Why would God warn only one man of the impending catastrophe? Why save only one family when there was gopher wood enough for a whole flotilla of arks?

Doubtless, these words suggest, God did try to warn others. From what the whole Bible teaches us about Him, we can be quite sure He told not only *some* others but *all* the others—that He pleaded and cautioned and pointed out over and over the way to escape disaster. What Genesis records is that one man heard.

And he heard, of course, because of that faithful daily walk. When the sun was shining and the birds singing and there seemed no reason for prayer and fasting and the other disciplines that kept him close to God, Noah nevertheless persisted. Companionship with God was habitual—and so when the saving word was spoken, Noah was able to receive it.

*He did all that God commanded him.* Noah not only heard God's instructions, he acted on them. Because of his long practice in obedience, the guidance he received was extremely specific: what, when, how.

But he did no more than God told him. There's a tendency in terrifying times—like Noah's, like ours—to see a flood rising everywhere we look. We become paranoid instead of purposeful: our doors are triple-locked, our basements stocked with survival food. *Some* kind of preparation is doubtless God's will for you; *every* kind of preparation isn't. God instructed Pharaoh to stockpile food in storehouses; for Noah to have done the same would have been useless. In one case drought was coming, in the other, rain—only God knew which. To try to prepare for the future without listening to Him can leave us paralyzed before all the things that "might happen." The "arks" in your life—the perfect protection and provision for the situations in which you will really find yourself—can be built only to His specific directions.

*And the waters increased, and bore up the ark.* Now an amazing thing happened: The same flood that swept away everything and everyone not centered in God, only served to float the ark higher. The torrents that destroyed others lifted Noah closer to Him.

Whatever the floods in your own life— bereavement, illness, financial loss—to ride them out with God means not simply survival, but a rising to new levels of commitment and trust.

Record in your "trip log" those times when seeming disaster was in fact the element that carried you—as the flood lifted the ark to the summit of

Ararat—to some new mountaintop in your experience of God.

*God remembered Noah.* When help seems long in coming, substitute your own name for Noah's. There must have been times in his lightless and confining quarters when Noah was sure God had forgotten him. The days when they had walked together on the solid earth and belonged to another world from this endless dripping on the roof, this ceaseless rocking on the floods of change and upheaval.

Change cuts us loose from our moorings, sets us adrift in a world from which every familiar landmark has vanished, where we question not only God's goodness but His very existence. Noah learned that God does not forget.

"I set my bow in the cloud." The covenant God makes with Noah as the flood subsides is "for all future generations": His rainbow shimmering through every storm, His promise that the rising water will not destroy.

*LORD, help me to see You in the rain as well as the sunshine.*

# 46      *Tunnels*

> *I will lead the blind in a way that they
> know not.... I will turn the darkness
> before them into light.*
>
> ISAIAH 42:16

*I* feel as if I'm in a long, black tunnel," the woman
wrote. The word *tunnel* jumped out at me—and I
knew why. My husband and I had recently spent
several months in Austria. Wherever we drove in
that mountainous land, the road led through
tunnels, some of them stretching so many miles
we'd begin to wonder if we'd ever see daylight
again.

But of course we would, bursting from the
blackness into the sunshine of a brand new
landscape. And looking back we'd see the jagged
outline of the formidable mountain through which
we'd just passed.

There were other ways across those mountains,
of course: We could have followed the old roads up
precipices, across snow fields, along narrow ledges.
But skilled engineers had devised a better way.

As I pray for this woman, I'm picturing God as the engineer and her dark tunnel as the way He has provided to speed her on her journey. I don't know what mountain of problems has plunged her into darkness. But I do know that the miles that seem so endless inside the tunnel are in fact the fastest way through: a marvel of road design through the barriers in our path.

*FATHER, help me to believe that the tunnel in my life today is the way Your love has forged.*

## 47    *Hidden Treasure*

*[GOD] will bring to light things now hidden in darkness.*
1 CORINTHIANS 4:5

*I*'m thinking this week about another kind of tunnel. Not tunnels that speed travelers on their way, but those that burrow deep into the earth in search of treasure.

I've been in this type of tunnel too. I've dropped in a hydraulic cage into the blackness of a coal mine in Kentucky. I've crawled down into gold diggings in Colorado, salt mines in Germany.

They're scary, these black, wet claustrophobic holes in the ground. But for centuries men have accepted the darkness and discomfort for the sake of what lies beneath the surface. Whether it's coal for power, salt for preservation, or gold for beauty, men have known that some things of great value can be reached only by going deep.

This week as I pray for the woman who wrote of her "dark tunnel," I'm picturing hidden treasure deep within her: resources of joy she's never tapped. I see how frightening the journey inward is, at times how painful.

In my prayers this week I see her tunnel as a mine shaft, sunk patiently by God beneath the surface of her life, probing down inch by inch, in spite of the fear, bringing hidden things to light, uncovering treasure she does not dream is there.

*FATHER, the tunneling hurts, but I trust the Miner.*

# 48     *Turmoil*

*I do not pray that thou shouldst take
them out of the world.*

JOHN 17:15

*I* love nature shows on television, not only for what they teach about the world around us, but for what they suggest about the world within.

In David Attenborough's "The Living Planet" series, we see a blue and sunlit stretch of the North Atlantic. Situated in the peaceful "eye" of circulating ocean currents, it's an area immune from gales and hurricanes—so calm that immense floating mats of Sargasso weed form on its unruffled surface. Through the seaweed scuttle tiny crabs and ... very little else. Few fish inhabit these crystal-clear waters, few birds pass overhead. This idyllic-looking region of the ocean is in fact a sterile world, lifeless and silent.

More than a thousand miles to the north is another sea. Shrouded in perpetual fog, swept by savage storms, it is the meeting place of the tropical Gulf Stream and the icy Labrador Current. Unlike the tranquil blue surface of the Sargasso Sea, these dark waters are in a constant froth of agitation. And so filled with fish that the ocean itself seems alive— millions upon millions of silvery shapes feeding on the plankton that in turn thrive on nutrients churned from the sea floor by the swirling water. Mammals are there too, herds of seal and humpback whales, while the air is dense with sea birds wheeling and diving into the richest feeding ground on earth.

Conflict, disturbance, sudden change—not so different, I thought, from the world we ourselves inhabit. Tumult and turmoil ... signs of Life itself.

*What courage this gives me, LORD: to know that the storms of the journey are none other than the stirrings of Your Spirit.*

*Journey's End:*

## Crossing Into the Kingdom

# 49 *Traveling Companion: JOSHUA ... who entered the Promised Land*

*The LORD your God is providing you a place of rest, and will give you this land.*

JOSHUA 1:13

We began our pilgrimage with God's word to Abraham: GO FROM! "Go from your country ... to a land that I will show you" (Gen. 12:1).

We end our journey with His command to Joshua: GO IN!

"Go in to take possession of the land which the Lord you God gives you to possess" (Josh. 1:11).

The journey of the spirit is not a mere sightseeing tour, but the entry procession into our rightful homeland.

Are we living as though we believe this? Or are we like the "shopping-bag lady" in New York City who survived for years on what she could scavenge from garbage cans. When she died, police discovered in her threadbare coat passbooks to bank accounts totalling nearly a quarter of a million dollars. We are heirs to all God's riches in Christ, yet we often live like paupers. We stand within sight of the Promised Land, but we do not enter. Joshua did, because he knew five secrets.

## 1. *Walking on two legs*

A one-legged man can't get far; neither can we if we leave either our part or God's part out of our stride. "YOU are to pass over this Jordan, to go in to TAKE possession of the land which the LORD your God GIVES you to possess." Does God give it or do we take it? Both, Joshua would say. It isn't either-or; it's both-and, like the left-right rhythm of a conquering army. "Be strong and of good courage" (that's our foot forward), "for the Lord your God is with you" (that's His).

## 2. *Divine timing*

"When you see the ark of the covenant of the Lord your God being carried by the Levitical priests, then you shall set out from your place and follow it" (Josh. 3:3). The ark, symbol of God's presence, always went ahead of the people of Israel.

Sometimes we get the order reversed and make a premature rush at the Promised Land. Maybe it's a healing that we think should come sooner than it does, or marriage when God still has some growing for us to do. In discouragement we conclude that particular promise just isn't for us: "I'll never get well." "I guess I'm just not meant to be married."

Forty years before the successful invasion under Joshua, the children of Israel, too, made an abortive attack on the Promised Land. "They presumed to go up ... although neither the ark of the covenant of the Lord, nor Moses, departed out of the camp. Then the Amalekites ... came down and defeated them" (Num. 14:44, 45).

### 3. Passing through water

"When the soles of the feet of the priests who bear the ark ... shall rest in the waters of the Jordan, the waters of the Jordan shall be stopped from flowing." Between the children of Israel and the Promised Land lay an impassable barrier, the Jordan River in spring spate.

Ask God what stands between you and full enjoyment of all He has for you. Is it fear of commitment? Of giving something up?

Joshua did not set about constructing a bridge— and our own efforts will not carry us across *our* Jordan. Instead, Joshua invited God right down into the threatening situation itself.

And when he did, the torrents of doubt and fear were checked. It didn't happen by magic. The temporary cutting off of the Jordan's flow has been observed in modern times, when spring floods undercut cliffs upstream, toppling tons of earth and rock into the river to create a natural dam. When we ask God *into* our fears and resistances, He involves us in His natural processes of change and transformation.

## 4. Stones from the riverbed

"Take up each of you a stone upon his shoulder … that this may be a sign among you … in time to come." That's the purpose of the log we've kept throughout our journey. God's marvelous guidance and provision is not to be forgotten when the immediate need is past, but kept before us as "a memorial for ever."

## 5. The edge of the sword

We're apt to shrink, nowadays, from the grisly details of Joshua's campaign, to find them primitive and bloodthirsty. What, after all, are we to make of God-fearing men who "utterly destroyed both men and women, young and old, oxen, sheep, and asses, with the edge of the sword"?

Precisely that they wanted God more than they wanted anything else. Reading ourselves into the account means identifying those "men and women, young and old, oxen and sheep" in our own lives. A "manly" refusal to admit need? A "ladylike" distaste for emotional displays? Some "innocent" small pleasure? Whatever it is, if it stands between us and God's promises, He wants it destroyed!

## The choice

Joshua's last words to his people make the perfect summary of our own eventful journey. An old man now, he reviews their long pilgrimage—and ours:

"Thus says the Lord ... I took your father Abraham from beyond the River and led him through all the land of Canaan ... and his children went down to Egypt.... I brought your fathers out of Egypt.... And you went over the Jordan."

In some or many areas of our lives we are living now in the Promised Land. Where we can relax, right? Not at all, cautions Joshua. The rest that God gives is not a relapse into carelessness. When we stop traveling, when we settle down, Joshua warns, two kinds of false gods will tempt us: "the gods your fathers served in the region beyond the River"—old idolatries, outgrown ways of dealing with problems, and "the gods of the Amorites in whose land you dwell"—the current standards of the world around us.

"Now therefore," Joshua concludes his farewell address, "choose *this day* whom you will serve." It is a daily matter, in the Promised Land as on the road, this decision to follow the God who has led us out of sorrow into joy.

*Help me each morning, LORD, to affirm with Joshua, "As for me and my house, we will serve the LORD!"*

50        *The Prism*

*From this time forth I make you hear new things, hidden things which you have not known.*

ISAIAH 48:6

When my friend Fran Horton came back from Germany she brought me a tiny crystal butterfly. I took it from its foam-lined box and held it to the lamplight the night she came over, marveling at the intricate facets. "Put it in a window where the sun will hit it," she advised.

Before going to bed I set it on a high sill in my study. Next morning, stepping into the room, I almost dropped my coffee cup.

The room pulsed with color.

A score of rainbows shimmered on walls, ceiling, desk top. The paper in the typewriter

153

glowed green and lilac. The cup in my hand, my hands themselves, held pools of color.

It was the same sunlight that streams into my study every morning. A prism of crystal was simply revealing what is always there.

Words can do that too ... help us see the hidden glory in ordinary things. A smile can do it. A kindness. A prayer.

We are living in the Promised Land, right now, this moment: that's what these things reveal. Even as we toil along the road, we are standing in the presence of the King. Even as we struggle to scale the heights, we are resting in His love.

*Thank You, LORD, for the crystalline moments in my life that show me the kingdom here and now.*

# 51 *The Promise*

> *The LORD has anointed me ... to give*
> *them a garland instead of ashes.*
> ISAIAH 61:1, 3

*U*gly! The recent lava flow was a smoldering black scar two miles wide and fifteen feet deep across the green Hawaiian landscape.

John stopped the car where lava blocked the road. Only the charred tops of trees poked out from the sullen wasteland before us. Twenty-one homes had been buried in the past two months as the sluggish flow inched down the East Rift zone of Kilauea Volcano. Family gardens, an orchid farm, papaya groves: nothing now but this desolation. Final as death.

Silently John turned the car around. It wasn't until hibiscus shrubs lined the road again that a lifeless weight seemed to lift from our own spirits. How bright Hawaii's flowers were, how lush the landscape!

"It's hard to believe," John said, "that all this beauty once looked like it does back there."

Hard to imagine ... but of course he was right! Every inch of these lovely Hawaiian Islands had been built by such catastrophic-seeming eruptions. Kilauea was simply continuing the process, adding land that would one day be as green and fertile as the banana groves we were passing now.

Dead? Yes, for the moment. Final? Of course not. All land, to the eye of faith, is Promised Land. This seeming desolation is the very place where love and joy and peace will spring in rich abundance.

*Thank You, FATHER, that every step of the journey with You is holy ground.*

## 52      *Forecast*

*For here we have no lasting city, but we seek the city which is to come.*
HEBREWS 13:14

*T*he weather forecast came over the radio the morning I was leaving Denver: sleet and freezing rain, with hazardous road conditions, for the upcoming weekend.

I'd tuned in to the local news and weather station each day of my Colorado stay; my writing assignment involved driving mountain roads in an unfamiliar car.

This time, though, I heard the dismal forecast with supreme detachment: I wouldn't be here when the predicted storm front moved in. My interest now was centered on what the weather would be like at home.

The information coming over the radio was doubtless accurate: the difference was in the reaction of the hearer. Reflecting on the experience, I thought I understood why the most God-centered people I know are also the most serene. They're not indifferent to the world's "weather," these modern saints. Of all people they are the most involved with the poor, the imprisoned, the environment, the peace movement.

But they're not frantic about them, as I so often get over these issues. They know that in the place where they'll spend tomorrow, there is no injustice, no lack, no war. They are strangers on earth, as I was in Colorado. Appreciating this world, rejoicing in its beauty, savoring it all the more because they know their stay is short.

*LORD, I'm so glad there are no clouds ... at Home.*

## 53 Travelers Aid ... Practicing Thanksgiving

*Enter his gates with thanksgiving.*
PSALM 100:4

*H*ow do we enter into all that His love has prepared for us? The psalmist provides the answer. When we approach God with grateful hearts, the gates of His kingdom swing wide. Three daily disciplines can make thanksgiving habitual. Try these stepping stones into the Promised Land.

### 1. Every day, surprise someone with a "thank-you"

The habit of gratitude starts at the human level—and surprise is the key. Excluded here is thanks that anyone can expect from you in the conventional course of things.

Our children used to enjoy a book about a little boy who visits a farm to thank the cow for his milk, the sheep for his sweater, and so forth. Adults too can use thanks to increase awareness of things we take for granted. Has the trash collector heard recently that you appreciate his faithfulness in all kinds of weather? If your breakfast melon tomorrow morning is rotten, you'll probably tell your grocer. Will you also let him know if it's especially good?

Opportunities to surprise people with thanks are all around us. What about the flower garden that gives you such pleasure on your way to work? When paying bills, why not clip a note to some item that turned out just as you hoped it would?

It was my friend Robert Updegraff who taught me about the "second thanks." When he received a book, for example, he'd write the customary thank-you note. But then when he finished it—perhaps months later—he'd write again, mentioning some passage he'd enjoyed.

Most of the time you won't know what effect your thanks has on the recipient—but you can be sure it will occasionally be greater than you dream. Meanwhile, the effect on you will be certain. You'll be training yourself day-by-day in seeking out the good and praiseworthy around you, rather than the more attention-grabbing evil.

## 2. Every day, thank God for something you have never until now thanked Him for

Thankfulness toward other people is a preparation for thankfulness to God. It's easier to feel grateful to other human beings, simply because their goodness to us is of necessity limited and specific. But from God "all blessings flow"—and in that "all" we can lose sight of the particular.

Each day will suggest its own thanksgiving. The gift of sight on a summer morning. Apples in cider time. Your warm blanket as nights grow cold. Thank Him for friends and family one by one. An inventory of your own body will reveal such marvels as fingers, knees, a tongue and the wonders of speech. When our children were small they took turns giving thanks at meals. One night the four-year-old's grace was: "Thank God for wallpaper." We've all enjoyed wallpaper more ever since.

The discipline of thanking God for a different blessing each day could be continued for a lifetime without repeating, for the thankful heart finds its capacity for appreciation multiplied.

*3. Every day, thank God for something about which you are not now happy*

This is both the hardest exercise in thanksgiving and the one that takes us deepest into the Promised Land. "Always and for everything giving thanks in the name of our Lord Jesus Christ to God the Father," wrote Paul to the Ephesians (Eph. 5:20). Advice to people enjoying great prosperity? On the contrary, the Christians in Ephesus were suffering privation and peril, and Paul was writing from prison!

Clearly, this kind of thanksgiving goes beyond simple thanks rendered for good received; it touches on the very structure of reality itself. We commonly think of thanksgiving as our response to a blessing from God. But what if it also works the other way? What if an attitude of thanksgiving for *everything* that comes to us is a first step in getting our hearts and minds in line with God's purposes, opening us to His goodness?

If you can stand before a financial setback, a disappointment, even death itself, and thank God for what in His hands this circumstance will become, you are acting out your conviction that the world is ultimately under His control.

Under each day's date in your trip log, describe the unwelcome situation for which you have in faith given thanks, leaving space after it for insights as they occur. A month, a year, even a lifetime may not be long enough to watch God bring to completion each event that you have entrusted to Him. But the practice of thanksgiving will allow you to say even as you wait, "Surely the Lord is in this place; and I did not know it" (Gen. 28:16).

Surely this everyday earth is the kingdom of God.

# Part II

## Special Journeys

*Thou madest us for thyself, and our heart is restless until it repose in Thee.*
*St. Augustine*

*Journey to Easter:*

*Road Map for Living*

# 54     *Eve of Holy Week*

*And they were on the road, going up to Jerusalem....*

MARK 10:32

*T*hey were on a journey, these first followers of Jesus, the journey to Easter. They had only hints of their destination on the eve of the week we now call holy. But they followed gladly because they had come to trust the One who led the way.

You and I make this journey to Easter, too, not this week only, but all our lives long—following Him again and again from death into life.

We have an advantage those earliest disciples did not have: We have a road map of the way ahead. They did not know the pitfalls that lay on the road to Easter. But because they followed to the end, the route is marked for us, the dangers known, the goal in sight.

Holy Week is the road map of our journey.

The days leading to that first Easter form a pattern that remains the same for every Christian pilgrim today. Those who experienced the wonder of the Resurrection had first to follow Jesus along the bewildering path of the previous week ... and so must we. Each day in Holy Week corresponds to a step in our walk toward the promise of God: beyond every ending a new beginning.

Each of us, of course, will be at a different place along the path. But each of us will find himself somewhere along the route. Whether it's Palm Sunday in your life, ringing with Hosannas; or Good Friday, dark with grief, the end of the road is the same: the empty tomb where what was lost has been given back, fuller and more glorious than before.

Those who walked that final week with Jesus did not know that unquenchable joy waited at the end of the road. We do know. And so we make the journey over these next eight days with the Easter song already on our lips.

*Allelujah! Thank You for those who walked this way before us.*

# 55　　*Palm Sunday*

*And the crowds ... shouted, "Hosanna
to the Son of David!"*
MATTHEW 21:9

*T*he cheering throngs, the waving palm branches
brought still more people crowding to the side of
the road. Those in front passed the news to those
behind: "Yes, riding a donkey!"

The loaded words spread swiftly. Five hundred
years earlier, Zechariah had foretold the restoration
of David's kingdom. The occupied nation had not
forgotten this prophecy, nor the manner in which
the son of David would enter Jerusalem—mounted
on a donkey.

At last, at last, the King had come! Tomorrow
they would be free from Rome's hated rule. Many
tore the very clothes from their backs and spread
them in the street for the animal to step on,
snatching them up again to be worn with pride at
the coming coronation. *See? I was there when He
entered Jerusalem!*

Holy Week begins as every Christian walk

begins, with Jesus coming into our lives. Our individual Palm Sunday may be as public as that first one: a religious rally, an eager crowd. For others, as it was for me, the event is quieter, more personal. But always a palm branch waves in our hearts: *He is here ... at last, at last!*

And once He has made His triumphal entry into our hearts, we experience "little Palm Sundays" all along the way. Each time we receive love or forgiveness—and recognize that it is God who is entering our lives in this way—we are once more standing on the royal road, welcoming the King. Palm Sunday represents all our personal encounters with God.

And only that. Some of the people who cried Hosanna on that first Palm Sunday mistook their personal experience for the whole of the truth. They had seen the Savior, they believed the matter was settled. They mistook the beginning for the end. They thought the struggle was behind them. In reality, the fiercest fight was just ahead.

*Allelujah! Thank You for coming into my life. Remind me how far we have to travel together.*

# 56 *Monday of Holy Week*

*And Jesus ... drove out all who sold
and bought in the temple, and he
overturned the tables of the
moneychangers and the seats of those
who sold pigeons.*

MATTHEW 21:12

*I*t was an unheard-of scandal! This young rabbi who
yesterday had the whole city in a patriotic uproar,
today stormed into the very temple precinct itself
and created chaos. Doves flapping, men shouting,
women scrabbling after the rolling coins. This
fellow from Galilee, once again stirring up trouble!

But stirring-up is always what happens when Jesus
enters the scene. Monday of Holy Week has its
parallel in our individual journey of faith. He
comes—and priorities are overturned, assumptions
swept aside. The first thing He did on entering
Jerusalem is the first thing He does on entering a life:
He goes straight to the temple—to the place where
we worship—and cleans out whatever is not part of
God's design. The process is called by many names:

sanctification, amendment of life, getting right with God; but the meaning is the same. The recognition that with Jesus in charge, many things we used to do, say, and want are no longer okay. It's such a common pattern that we've come to expect it.

And there's the danger in the Monday experience. We think we know what things He disapproves of. When my mother was growing up, the list included wearing makeup, reading novels and riding a bicycle on Sunday. Each group, each era, has its own expectations.

But the hallmark of that Monday in Jerusalem was surprise. Weren't sacrificial doves prescribed in the Law of Moses? Weren't the moneychangers performing a needed service—exchanging a score of currencies into standard temple coinage? "Astonished" is how Mark describes people's reactions to that original cleansing, and astonished is how we feel when God's housecleaning—not the one we envisaged—gets underway within us. Prejudice. Old hurts. A sense of inferiority. Whatever blocks our relationship with Him, out it must go.

"What are You doing?" we cry when the Cleanser strides in.

"I'm making myself a temple," He replies.

*Allelujah! Take from the altar of my heart all that cannot worship You.*

# 57  Tuesday of Holy Week

*And he was teaching daily in the temple.*
LUKE 19:47

*T*here was room in the temple courtyard now. With the money tables gone, the baskets carted off, the great court was quiet, open. And into that vacated space the people poured to hear Him.

That's how it is in the Tuesdays of our lives. When His housecleaning clears away the clutter and opens up room—in our schedules, in our hearts— then we hunger to fill the vacuum with knowledge of Him. This third day of Holy Week corresponds to the times in our lives when we drive two hundred miles to hear an inspired preacher, when we go without lunch to buy the latest teaching tape, or spend our week's vacation at a church retreat.

What teaching it was, there in the temple! Jesus saw a widow drop a penny into the treasury, and taught about sacrificial giving. He was shown a coin with Tiberius's profile, and taught about priorities.

But Tuesday is not yet Easter Sunday. That is the

risk on this part of our walk—that we'll be content with head knowledge and fail to complete the journey. All of us know people who stop at Tuesday. They attend three weekly Bible studies, run from conference to conference—and never encounter the risen Lord.

Tuesday is an especially dangerous day for me. I love study just for the sake of study. The sight of a fresh notebook makes my pulses speed. I can take beautifully outlined notes of a lecture without relating a word the speaker says to my own life. There must have been many like me who heard Jesus teach that first Holy Week. There were crowds in the temple, only a handful at the empty tomb.

But Jesus will not let us stop short of Easter, not forever. The time comes to close the books, to leave the lecture hall. To take the road to Calvary and beyond.

*Allelujah! Thank You for the teaching that sets us on the way.*

# 58 *Wednesday of Holy Week*

*And the blind and the lame came to
him in the temple, and he healed them.*
MATTHEW 21:14

*M*ind and body. Reason and miracle. Jesus'
ministry included both, this final week as always. In
the clean-swept temple He taught and He also
healed. He asked men to understand, and He
performed what surpasses understanding. As the
blind saw and the lame walked, cries of wonder
echoed along the marble porticoes, and the crowd
swelled till temple authorities took fresh alarm.
Even more than brilliant teaching, miracles will
always draw throngs. Wednesday's miracles of
healing kept the city in a fever of excitement.

I've felt that excitement on the Wednesdays of
my own life. I've seen it in the great arenas where
today's charismatic healers draw their thousands.
I've known the ecstatic gratitude of seeing my
husband John instantaneously healed of cancer. This
fourth day in Holy Week represents those times

when our natural lives touch the supernatural. When here on earth we are caught up in the divine mystery.

But still we are not at the best. We stand wonder-struck but short of Easter. How strange it is, this journey we're embarked on. On Wednesday we seem to have arrived at the very throne room of God—and yet the road leads on, out into the dark.

How many of those who were healed there in the temple followed Jesus to the end? "Though he had done so many signs before them," John writes of that last week, "yet they did not believe in him" (John 12:37). For Jesus, healing was always a sign, a pointer to something greater and better.

Better than health? Greater than an end to pain? Yes, He answers, follow Me and see! Unspeakable pain lay just ahead for Jesus, but He embraced it for the sake of that better thing. The road to Easter does not remain on the mountaintop of miracle. It leads down, through death to life everlasting.

*Allelujah! Thank You for the healing that points beyond.*

# 59 *Maundy Thursday*

*Peter said to him, "Even if I must die*
*with you, I will not deny you." And so*
*said all the disciples.*

MATTHEW 26:35

*T*he triumphal entry into Jerusalem. The cleansing
of the temple. The teaching, the miracles. All
displayed their leader's power, and the faith of the
disciples soared. Now, on this fifth day of the week,
came the most intimate moment of all: the Passover
meal, that high holy feast, just the twelve and Jesus.
Over and over, at table, He reiterated His love for
them, even kneeling before them to wash their
travel-weary feet.

If they'd ever doubted, they could no longer do
so. What if, as Jesus cautioned, testings and trials lay
just ahead? They could face anything. "Lord," Peter
assured Him, "I am ready to go with you to prison
and to death" (Luke 22:33).

Maundy Thursday corresponds to those times in
our own lives when our faith feels unassailable.
Surrounded by so many proofs of His love, how
could we ever doubt?

Thursday is the most perilous day of our pilgrimage.

Because, when the test comes, we so often fail. Before daybreak Peter was swearing he'd never heard of Jesus. Maundy Thursday represents both our moments of highest commitment and our most grievous failures. The times when, having made great promises, we fall on our faces. When we let God down and let ourselves down and are left with only the certainty of our own weakness.

Yet strangely, Thursday also ushers in the most hopeful stage of our journey. Because at last we are truly on the road to Easter. We have learned better than to place our trust in ourselves. "I tell you, Peter," Jesus replied to Peter's confident boast, "the cock will not crow this day, until you three times deny that you know me" (Luke 22:34).

But He said it without condemnation, without rejection. Jesus knew that the way leads through loss. Loss of self-satisfaction and self-sufficiency. He knew that on the other side of Easter, Peter would find the power that never fails.

*Allelujah! Thank You that the strength is Yours alone.*

## 60    *Good Friday*

*And they crucified him.*
MARK 15:24

*I*t was the darkest day. The unbearable day. Many who had followed Jesus up to now fled from the events of Friday. And those who stayed to watch wept in horror.

The rigged trial, the mob howling for the blood of the Man who had failed to meet their patriotic expectations. The brutal beating, the savagery of the soldiers, the stumbling walk through the city He had entered to cheers five days before. Finally, the nails pounded into flesh, the tortured body jerked upright, the naked Man dying by inches as His enemies jeered.

To have it end like this, after all the bright promise! It was not just the cruel death of the disciples' young leader, but the death of their faith, the end of all they believed in, on this black Friday that seemed anything but good.

Most of us have experienced this Friday for ourselves. It's not the disillusionment of Thursday, when our own performance falls short. It's the blow that strikes from outside, the tragedy that destroys our loved one, our health, our livelihood. We feel, as the disciples did on that terrible day, that Jesus himself has failed us. If He were really God's Son, things like this could not happen. "Are you not the Christ? Save yourself and us!" (Luke 23:39).

There is no way around the Fridays of our lives, only the way through—through pain and death and burial. As His sorrowing followers laid Jesus in the tomb, so we lay down the wreckage of our hope. Ahead was Easter Sunday, but on Friday they couldn't know that. And neither can we in the first shock of loss. We can only know that we *will* know. We can only know that the whole story is not yet told.

For, of course, Jesus *is* the Christ. He *is* saving us, whatever the appearance. He is bringing about our everlasting joy in a way only God could have chosen. If it is Friday in your life today, Easter cannot be far away.

*Allelujah! In the darkness I detect You, for You went into the darkness for me.*

# 61  *Holy Saturday*

*On the sabbath they rested according to
the commandment.*

LUKE 23:56

*A*fter the din and tumult of that terrifying Friday
came this day of absolute silence. It was the
Sabbath, the day of rest. No clatter of hooves came
from the deserted streets, no sing-song of water
sellers.

Behind some of those shuttered doorways the
silence was doubly deep. Here and there, in homes
about the city, Jesus' former followers huddled in a
stillness, not of reverence, but of the grave. For
them all was finished. The future had been buried
with their leader; they had nothing more to live for.

More than once in my own life I have
wondered: Which is harder, the day of disaster or
the day that follows? During an emergency we
experience the rush of adrenalin, the numbness of
shock. But what is there to sustain us in the empty
aftermath when our joy has died but we must go on
living? Holy Saturday is that dark tunnel where we

find ourselves when the light of faith goes out.

To keep us going when there seems to be no point to it—that is the wisdom of religious tradition. What did Jesus' devastated followers do on that silent Saturday? They kept the letter of the Law. They observed the Sabbath. There can't have been much conviction, for them, behind this weekly formality. They had only habit to get them through the hours.

But they did have habit. "Going through the motions" is usually condemned as meaningless for the walk of faith. Going to church when we no longer believe, reciting prayers we no longer mean. But when such things are all we can do, the motions of faith can keep us going ... until the meaning comes.

*Allelujah! Thank You for the polestar of discipline in the nighttime of the soul.*

## 62 *Easter Sunday*

*He is not here; for he has risen.*
MATTHEW 28:6

$O$nly a week had passed since that triumphant Palm Sunday entrance into Jerusalem—but what a difference in the little procession that set out now! No cheering crowds, no waving branches. Just a few silent women setting out in the gray dawn to perform the last sad rites at the tomb.

The day that changed human history was not a public occasion but a private one. The day when everlasting life broke into earthly time began not with celebration but with tears.

This is still the way Easter breaks into our lives—when we least expect it, when all seems lost. That's when the stone rolls away and the angel speaks and "death is swallowed up in victory" (1 Cor. 15:54).

If it seems too good to be true, this joy that invades our hearts, it seemed so on that first Easter morning too. Mary Magdalene could not believe what her eyes were telling her; she took Jesus to be a gardener at work early among the graves. Preoccupied with her loss, she barely glanced at the figure standing before her on the path. She had a mournful task to fulfill and—

"Mary."

There in the first light of dawn, Mary stood still. That voice ... that tone of loving involvement ...

This was the moment, the moment when Jesus called her by name, that Easter broke like the sunrise into her heart. It is how we recognize Him still. The risen Jesus calls us so personally, comes into our lives so individually, that with Mary Magdalene, we can only cry out in glad recognition.

And then we do what the women did on that first Easter Sunday. Dropping their spices and ointments, the burdens of their sad errand, they rushed to tell the others.

They set the pattern, these women who were first at the empty tomb—the twofold pattern of the Christian faith newborn that Easter morning. They met the living Jesus. And they brought the good news to those who grieved.

That's always our role when it's Easter in our lives: to tell someone else that He is risen.

*Allelujah! Allelujah! Allelujah!*

*Pentecost:*

*Journeying
with the Spirit*

# 63 Friday Before Pentecost: The Promise

*For the promise is to you and to your children.*

ACTS 2:39

*M*idway through the Christian year comes the great Feast of Pentecost.

For the first six months of the church calendar we trace the events of Jesus' earthly life from His advent to His ascension into heaven. For the second half of the year we focus on the difference all of this makes in our daily lives.

For it *does* make a difference to you and me. And the difference is the Holy Spirit.

The Spirit was not new, of course, on the Day of Pentecost. It was the everlasting Spirit who presided over creation. Nor was this the first time the Spirit appeared in human history. All through the Old Testament the Holy Spirit is recognized as the source of unusual power. The Spirit gave strength to Israel's heroes. The Spirit spoke through the prophets.

But that's just it ... These rare manifestations of the Spirit of God were reserved for the few: for kings and sages and holy men. The great mass of mankind could know God only secondhand.

And then around the year 400 B.C. one of these Spirit-inspired men uttered astonishing words:

> *"And it shall come to pass afterward,*
> *that I will pour out my spirit on all flesh....*
> *Even upon the menservants and*
> *maidservants in those days, I will pour out*
> *my spirit." (Joel 2:28, 29)*

*Afterward* ... *When* this would be, and *after* what, not even the prophet Joel could guess. Who could imagine God becoming man, living a human life, dying an inhuman death?

But the unimaginable happened. After Jesus' resurrection He reminded the disciples of the promise made four centuries earlier: "You shall receive power when the Holy Spirit has come upon you" (Acts 1:8).

It must have seemed too marvelous to believe, that the Spirit who had empowered kings would come to a group of humble fishermen. But God had promised, and so in faith the disciples asked, as Jesus' followers have asked ever since.

> *Come down, O Love divine,*
> *Seek thou this soul of mine ...*

*O Comforter, draw near,*
*Within my heart appear.*

> *—Bianco da Siena, 1367*

*HOLY SPIRIT, prepare my heart for Your*
*coming.*

# 64 *Eve of Pentecost: Something Better*

*It is to your advantage that I go away.*

JOHN 16:7

*T*omorrow is the big day! Pentecost itself! Have
you mailed your Pentecost cards? Baked? Decorated
your home?

Neither have I. Even in many churches, tomorrow there will be only token observance of this first
and greatest anniversary in Christian history.

Early Christians, were they to join us at church
tomorrow, would be baffled by our lack of
excitement. For the first few centuries there were
only two dates on the Christian calendar: Easter and

Pentecost. Advent, Christmas, Epiphany, Lent and all the rest were unknown. Christians honored just the two fundamental facts of our faith.

Jesus rose from the dead.

Jesus sent His Spirit to be with us.

The day the Spirit came—the Day of Pentecost— was forever afterward observed not only as "the birthday of the Church" but as a day of rejoicing for each individual believer. "It is to your advantage that I go away," Jesus told His disciples (John 16:7).

Could there be anything better, those first follow-ers of His must have asked, than to have Jesus with them? His actual physical presence in their midst?

Yes, Jesus insisted. "For if I do not go away," He explained, "the Counselor will not come to you; but if I go, I will send him to you" (John 16:7).

Pentecost is the day the Counselor came. And ever since, Christians have affirmed Jesus' words: It *is* to our advantage. In hundreds of hymns across the centuries they've acclaimed the day that brought us something better.

> *Spirit of mercy, truth and love,*
> *O shed thine influence from above;*
> *And still from age to age convey*
> *The wonders of this sacred day.*
> *—Author unknown, 1774*

*HOLY SPIRIT, preside over this joyful birthday celebration.*

## 65 Day of Pentecost: The Gift of Courage

*When the day of pentecost had come,
they were all together in one place.*

ACTS 2:1

$A$ll of them together—Jesus' mother, the eleven
remaining disciples, an assortment of other men
and women—120 people in all. A mere remnant of
the throngs who had flocked to see Jesus during His
earthly lifetime.

The "one place" was probably that same
upper room in Jerusalem where Jesus had eaten the
Last Supper with His friends. In the seven weeks
since that fateful night, they'd been rocked by
events almost too momentous to grasp: their
Leader's death ... His resurrection ... finally His
ascension into heaven, leaving them alone now and
afraid.

Jerusalem was a dangerous place for followers
of the executed rabbi. The city swarmed with
government spies and temple informers. But Jesus
had given His followers an order before He left

them: "He charged them not to depart from Jerusalem, but to wait for the promise of the Father" (Acts 1:4). And so they stayed on in the risky city, clustering together in the upper room, waiting for they scarcely knew what.

Then it happened! It was a festive holy day in Jerusalem, the great Jewish feast of Pentecost. "And they were all filled with the Holy Spirit" (Acts 2:4).

All. Not just Peter and John and the other leaders, but all 120. Filled with joy, peace, love … and a strange new confidence. They burst from the room where they'd been hiding, into the crowded streets of the city. Instead of speaking of Jesus among themselves in whispers, they buttonholed everyone they met, bubbling over with their love for Him.

Peter, who a few weeks earlier had tried to placate a mob by pretending he'd never heard of Jesus, delivered a no-holds-barred oration. "This Man *you* killed," he told the astonished crowd, "was the Messiah sent by God! You saw the amazing things He did, so don't try to excuse yourselves!"

Hard-hitting words. Effective words. By the end of the Day of Pentecost, those original 120 Christians had become more than three thousand.

What had turned weak people into strong ones? The same Spirit who can take our self-centered, fear-filled lives today, and make them glorious.

*Hail this joyful day's return,*
*Hail the Pentecostal morn,*
*Morn when our ascended Lord*
*On His Church His Spirit poured!*
      *—Hilary of Poitiers, fourth century*

*HOLY SPIRIT, this season of Pentecost let me*
*take my faith out of hiding.*

# 66    *First Sunday After Pentecost: The Gift of Grace*

> *For the law was given through Moses;*
> *grace and truth came through Jesus*
> *Christ.*
>
> JOHN 1:17

*T*he streets of Jerusalem onto which those 120 new-minted evangelists erupted were even more packed than usual. From all over the known world pilgrims had thronged to the Holy City for the ancient festival of Pentecost. Observed fifty days after Passover (*pente* means *fifty* in Greek), this was the day when Jews celebrated the giving of the Law on Mount Sinai.

What a momentous event that had been! The most significant in the Jews' long history: the point at which a frightened group of runaway slaves had become a nation. And so the faithful had come to Jerusalem on this Day of Pentecost twelve hundred years later—from Egypt, from Persia, from Rome. It was the Law that drew these diverse races and cultures together. The Law that gave them their common identity and their strength.

But now, here in Jerusalem on this particular Pentecost, an even greater event had occurred. The giving, not of the Law, but of the Spirit. The forging not of a nation, but of a church that would include all nations.

The Law had laid down a set of rules that showed people how to live. "The law was our custodian," as Paul put it, "until Christ came" (Gal. 3:24).

Now, with the coming of the Spirit at Pentecost, those rules were henceforth to be inscribed not on tablets of stone but on the human heart. The Spirit was to achieve what the Law could never in fact accomplish: implant Jesus' own mind and will in you and in me.

*Breathe on me, Breath of God,*
*Fill me with life anew,*
*That I may love what Thou dost love,*
*And do what Thou wouldst do.*
*—Edwin Hatch, 1866*

HOLY SPIRIT, *what will You have me do*
*today?*

# 67    *Second Sunday After Pentecost: The Gift of Communication*

*Each one heard them speaking in his*
*own language.*
ACTS 2:6

*I*t was the first thing the crowd in Jerusalem's streets noticed about these Christians on whom the Spirit had fallen. They made sense! These people speaking with such conviction about Jesus were, most of them, from Galilee. Yet their hearers—

speakers of Arabic, Greek, Latin, Persian; all of that polyglot throng—heard them "telling in our own tongues the mighty works of God" (v. 11).

Whether the miracle occurred in the mouths of the speakers or in the ears of the hearers, scholars debate to this day. Perhaps it was both ... the miracle that occurs every time two people communicate. Every time we hear, really *hear,* what someone else is saying. Every time we get across what we mean, leaping out of our isolation to touch soul to soul.

It's a sign that the Spirit dwells within us, this ability to "speak one another's language." It's most dramatic when the leap is made, as it was on that Day of Pentecost, across foreign cultures. But it's no less marvelous when a bridge is built across generations or social backgrounds to the teenager at the breakfast table, or the woman at the office.

How often I forget to ask the Spirit's aid at these times! How frequently I "witness" to others and get a blank stare in return. How often I close my ears when others speak!

For years, for instance, I was deaf to the words "Are you saved?" Maybe I'd heard them too often, or maybe I'd formed judgments about people who used that phrase, but those syllables never got past my outer ear. Until one day I listened to the meaning behind the words ... and stepped into a whole new dimension of God's love.

Just as, on that Day of Pentecost, the anniversary of the Giving of the Law became for Christians the anniversary of the Giving of the Spirit, so another Old Testament memory—the breakdown of understanding at the Tower of Babel—was transformed by the Spirit into the marvel of comprehension.

> *In Salem's street was gathered*
> *A crowd from many a land,*
> *And all in their own tongues*
> *Did the Gospel understand;*
> *For by the triumph of the Son*
> *The curse of Babel was undone.*
>
> —*George Timms, 1910*

> *HOLY SPIRIT, let me hear You in the words of others today ... and they in mine.*

# 68 *Third Sunday After Pentecost: The Gift of Guidance*

> *They attempted to go into Bithynia, but the Spirit of Jesus did not allow them.*
>
> ACTS 16:7

*P*aul and Timothy are on a missionary journey, bringing the good news of salvation. But not hit or miss. They don't blunder from place to place simply in the hope that they'll find listeners. Jesus himself is with them. Day by day, moment by moment, He instructs them. *Go* here. *Speak* there. *Keep silent* somewhere else. He points out the people He wants to reach, the resting places He has chosen for them.

But—something extraordinary is going on! Paul and Timothy have never laid eyes on Jesus. They never knew the young Galilean carpenter whose ministry they're carrying forward. This is more than twenty years after that Man was executed—probably before Timothy was born.

And yet ... *Jesus is with them.* Encouraging,

correcting, guiding. And at the same moment back in Jerusalem, down in Cyprus, in a hundred other villages and towns, other Christians are experiencing the same reality. *Jesus is with us!* He is *here,* close as a heartbeat, leading each of us step by step on our separate paths.

How is this possible? How can He be in so many places at once, attending so individually to each need? The answer, of course, is His Spirit, no longer confined to a single body, no longer bound by the physics of earthly existence.

For time, of course, is no more a barrier to the Spirit than space. All over the world today, Christians know the same inner nudge, the same silent Voice that guided Paul and Timothy.

Some years ago my husband and I set out on our own small missionary journey. We chose Africa because we knew so little about it: For an entire year we experimented to see if the Spirit still guides today.

He does! He led us to the countries, the people, the needs that we could never have contacted on our own. Because we were in strange settings, we asked Him about everything—what to eat, whom to speak to, where to stop for the night—and learned that nothing is too small or mundane for His involvement.

"It is to your advantage that I go away" (John 16:7), Jesus told His disciples. For by going away in physical form, He came to be with us in Spirit always and everywhere.

*Come, gracious Spirit, heavenly Dove,*
*With light and comfort from above;*
*Be Thou our guardian, Thou our guide,*
*O'er every thought and step preside.*
                    *—Simon Browne, 1680–1732*

*HOLY SPIRIT, forgive me for the steps I take*
*without asking of You the way.*

## 69    *Fourth Sunday After Pentecost: The Gift of Love*

> *This is my commandment, that you love one another.*
> JOHN 15:12

*I*t sounds so simple; it turns out to be so hard! To love *some* others, sure: Some people are easy to love. But if you knew a certain individual in *my* family … *my* office … *my* neighborhood! To treat these people decently, to be civil, to accord them their rights—that, with great self-control, I may manage.

But to *love* them? The selfish, the arrogant? God alone could love some of the people I have to deal with!

And God alone does—His Spirit within me—making me capable of what I myself could never do. This is what drew the multitudes to those first Christians: their love for one another. "Now the company of those who believed were of one heart and soul, and no one said that any of the things which he possessed was his own" (Acts 4:32).

Were those first Christians perhaps naturally more generous, than people in the twentieth century? It certainly didn't sound that way during Jesus' lifetime, as they bickered over who was greatest!

But here they were, putting others' interests ahead of their own. "There was not a needy person among them" (Acts 4:34), onlookers wonderingly reported.

And not only poverty began to disappear among the little band of believers, but disease as well! Wherever these first Christians went, healing followed. But … these Christians praying so willingly for the well-being of total strangers—these were the same men who not so long ago had wanted to call down fire from heaven to consume those who didn't belong to their tight little circle.

What had happened to the cantankerous group who had followed the rabbi from Nazareth?

Pentecost had happened. The coming of Jesus' Spirit, not as an external presence issuing commandments too hard for ordinary humans to follow, but as the power to keep those commandments, welling up from deep inside. From the time of that first Pentecost, Christians have made the wondrous discovery: not that we have become more loving, but that we have made room for Him.

*Come, Holy Spirit, heavenly Dove,*
*With all Thy quickening powers;*
*Kindle a flame of sacred love*
*In these cold hearts of ours.*
                    *—Isaac Watts, 1707*

*HOLY SPIRIT, use my feet and hands and voice to love the people You bring to me today.*

## 70     *Fifth Sunday After Pentecost: The Gift of Jesus*

> *When the Counselor comes ... he will*
> *witness to me.*
> JOHN 15:26

*H*ow the writers of the Bible struggle to convey
their experience of the Spirit! Writing about the Day
of Pentecost, Luke can only say the Spirit came "like
the rush of a mighty wind" (Acts 2:2).

Wind. Image of immense power, and yet ...
elusive, too. Strong ... but invisible, unpredictable.

Of the three Persons of the Trinity, people have
always had the hardest time describing this one. His
very name, Holy Spirit, Holy Ghost, suggests
something formless, ineffable. God the Father fills
the mind with concrete pictures—the earthly father
we had or would like to have had. God the Son has
a human form, a thousand physical settings where
we meet Him, from the manger in Bethlehem to the
Cross of Calvary.

But God the Spirit? Artists most often portray Him as a dove, the form in which John the Baptist saw Him descend upon Jesus. A shy and gentle bird that flutters out of reach when you try to grasp it? A strange image of Almighty God!

The titles the Bible gives Him—Counselor, Helper, Advocate, Comforter—tell what He does, not who He is. It's as though, when God comes to us as Spirit, He chooses to remain out of sight. It's as though He wants our attention somewhere else.

Which, of course, He does. "When the Counselor comes ..." Jesus told His followers, "He will bear witness to *me*."

That is the Spirit's first and most constant function: to show us Jesus. He wants us to know Jesus as the One who strengthens and guides and lets us do the Father's will. The Spirit comes to us not as an addition to our faith in Christ but as its source. "No one can say 'Jesus is Lord,'" says St. Paul, "except by the Holy Spirit" (1 Cor. 12:3).

> *O Spirit of Life, O Spirit of God,*
> *Increase our faith in our dear Lord;*
> *Unless Thy grace the power should give,*
> *None can believe in Christ and live.*
> —*Johann Niedling, 1602–1668*

*HOLY SPIRIT, show me Jesus today ... and each day throughout these six months of Pentecost.*

*Advent:*

*Journey to
Bethlehem*

# 71  *Saturday Before Advent Sunday*

*Surely I am coming soon. Amen.*
*Come, Lord Jesus!*
REVELATION 22:20

$T$he four weeks of preparation for Christmas: what a strange, contradictory season!

We're turning the last pages on the calendar

... and the church says the year is just beginning.

The event we celebrate happened 2,000 years ago

... and the church calls our attention to the future.

It's a time of eager expectation: angel choirs and "tidings of great joy"

... and the church drapes itself in mourning.

They're the most hectic weeks of the year: more activity, more expenses, more pressures

... and the church announces Peace on Earth.

The shortest days come now: the longest, darkest nights

 ... and the church proclaims it the Season of Light.

The dictionary defines *paradox* as "a statement that is seemingly contradictory, yet true." Christians through the ages have affirmed that the paradoxes of Advent are in fact true—the greatest truths we know.

It is only when we try to eliminate one extreme or the other, to pick and choose the elements of truth that appeal to us, that we miss the totality of what God is doing among us.

"Truth," wrote the Danish theologian Soren Kierkegaard, "is the tension between paradoxes." This Advent let us seek the meaning of Christmas in the very tensions of the season themselves. In the noise as well as the Silent Night. In the darkness as well as the light of the star.

*Come* is the root meaning of the word *Advent*. Let us prepare for His coming into this world of paradox.

*Come, LORD JESUS, over these next four weeks, into every part of our Christmas preparation.*

# 72 *First Sunday in Advent: The Paradox of Solemn Joy*

*And Mary said, "Behold, I am the handmaid of the Lord."*
LUKE 1:38

*H*appy New Year!

The secular New Year, January 1, can fall on any day of the week. But for Christians each year begins, as each week begins, on a Sunday.

What a strange subdued Sunday this Christian New Year is! In our local Episcopal church the folding panels behind the altar are closed, hiding the painting of Jesus Transfigured. There are no flowers on the altar. The pulpit cloth is purple, the color of mourning. Is this any way to welcome in the new year?

"Yes," believers over the centuries have answered. Beginnings, real beginnings, are like that. Painful … hidden. No dance bands. No noisemakers and confetti. True beginnings happen in silence and in secret. The seed sprouting in the earth. The idea germinating in the mind.

Nor at the moment of beginning can we ever know the outcome. That's the reason for the blank and shuttered wall behind the altar. As the baby stirred in Mary's womb she could not foresee the events of the Life she was bringing into the world. As John the Baptist called the crowds to repentance, he did not know which one among them would prove to be the promised Messiah.

And beginnings, real beginnings, involve death. The death of the grain of wheat so that a new crop can grow. The death of false idols to make room for the true.

Advent summons us to die to the old as we await the birth of the new. To examine our hearts and put to death anything there that cannot welcome the Child in the manger.

As we prepare for Christmas during these next four weeks, let's watch for signs of death to the old self-centered life. A smile for the others in the long line at the post office. An extra bit of patience with a slow salesperson. A gift for someone others may forget. It's not a spectacular way to celebrate. No crowds will gather in Times Square to cheer. But in heaven angels will sing.

Happy New Year!

*In this season of expectation, LORD, give us Mary's humble, hopeful heart.*

# 73 Second Sunday in Advent: The Paradox of the Cross at the Crib

*She will bear a son, and you shall call his name Jesus, for he will save his people from their sins.*

MATTHEW 1:21

*L*ike many families, we've picked up Advent traditions over the years. Such as setting up our creche set three weeks before Christmas. Only the stable goes on the mantelpiece this early, with the shepherds and sheep nearby. Mary and Joseph are still a long way from Bethlehem—on the other side of the room—and the Wise Men remain upstairs (they won't reach the stable until the feast of the Epiphany on January 6).

Something else goes in the stable today, though: a small wooden cross beside the manger where the Baby will go on Christmas Eve.

We added the cross to the set twenty-five years ago. That was the year I wrote a children's book called *Our Christmas Story* with Mrs. Billy Graham. Meant to be read aloud in Advent, the book begins not in Bethlehem, but in the Garden of Eden, and follows the whole human story—from the time we drew apart from God to the stable where He drew close to us.

The publisher seemed happy with the concept—until the time came to design the cover. We all agreed on a manger scene. "With a cross, of course," Ruth Graham said, "behind the crib."

The editor was horrified, the artist aghast. A cross? At Christmas? And on a children's book! Children would never understand. Anyhow, Christmas should be a happy time!

"Yes, but what are we happy about?" Ruth asked quietly. "Not just His birth. That alone changed nothing for you and me." It was the cross, she explained, that made the difference. "It was in order to die that He was born."

And of course when the cross appeared on the cover, children understood perfectly. Pain and comfort, laughter and tears, wandering from home and being found again ... it's we adults who make opposites of these things. The cross in our crib set reminds us of a mystery: He was born in order to die. He died in order that we might be born to everlasting life.

*Thank You, LORD, for accepting the shadow of my sin across Your holy crib.*

# 74    *Third Sunday in Advent: The Paradox of the Long-expected Surprise*

> *The Son of man is coming at an unexpected hour.*
>
> LUKE 12:40

*I*f Jesus tarries," Mr. Weber would say, "I'll come again Tuesday."

He was an odd-jobs man who, in fact, came to our house every Tuesday for many years. As a child I always wondered if he wanted Jesus to come before next week or not—for as he put up screens or repaired my bicycle bell, he whistled like a man who was totally content. One thing I was sure of: For Mr. Weber, the imminent appearance of Jesus was as daily a fact as the weather. Unpredictable, like tomorrow's sunshine, but certain to occur before long.

When, years later, I took some Scripture courses, I discovered that Mr. Weber's expectant attitude was also the Bible's. The New Testament has little to say about the birth of Jesus—only St. Luke's Gospel gives any space to it—but it has a very great deal to say about the Second Coming. For two thousand years the church has maintained the same emphasis, urging believers to watch with "feet shod and lamps lit."

Advent was the season the early church set aside to contemplate Jesus' coming in glory, as King of Kings. If we find it somehow easier to think about His coming in humility, as a Baby in a manger, that's understandable. The birth of a baby is a human-sized event. We can picture it, relate to it.

How can we relate to an event of cosmic proportion, a day without a date? It will come, Jesus tells us, when we least expect it. Not when a century ends or a comet lights the sky, though at such times people have always rushed to the mountaintops to await Him. That's not the way He tells us to keep Advent.

He says that when He comes He wants to find us doing the work He has given us to do. Putting up screens and repairing bells. Now, in December, shopping and wrapping and baking. If He comes tonight, may He find us discharging such small errands of love. Preparing our great Christmas celebration two weeks from now ... if Jesus tarries.

*LORD, help us to live each day in joyful anticipation of Your appearing.*

# 75 *Fourth Sunday in Advent: The Paradox of Light in Darkness*

*The light shines in the darkness, and the darkness has not overcome it.*

JOHN 1:5

*T*onight we light the fourth and final candle in our Advent wreath. The first candle, lit on New Year's Day, the first Sunday of Advent, is little more than a purple stub. Each Sunday we've added another, until now in this darkest week of the year, our wreath is its brightest.

It's another of the Advent traditions we share with Christians all over the Northern Hemisphere. And like so many Christian customs, its roots are very old, tapping human experiences we might have forgotten if faith had not claimed them for her own.

Our wreath with its base of evergreens takes me back to the dark forests of Europe, where families, wrapped in animal skins against the cold, watched in terror as the sun rose less high each day, lingered less long in the sky. I picture a wheel to represent the sun built in a clearing, and watch the shivering people build fires around the rim in a desperate effort to call back the light and warmth.

Why do we Christians celebrate Jesus' birth in December? The actual month is not recorded in the Bible, but it was probably springtime, lambing season in Judea, the only time shepherds remained in the fields at night.

But when the church settled on a date to commemorate His coming—His coming in time, His coming at the end of time—it chose not spring but this darkest hour of the year. In replacing the ancient midwinter ceremonies with the Advent celebration, it did what Christianity has always done: spoke God's word into the fear-filled pagan world.

It is not what men do, Advent tells us, that brings back the light. Not our fires, our candles, even our prayers. The initiative is always God's. When things are darkest, when times are hardest, when the case is most hopeless: Look up! Someone is coming into our need ... and now He is very close indeed.

*LORD, thank You for coming in the nighttime of our lives.*

# 76    *Christmas Eve: The Paradox of Peace in Pandemonium*

*And all went to be enrolled, each to his
own city. And Joseph also went up
from Galilee ... to Bethlehem ... to be
enrolled with Mary, his betrothed, who
was with child.*

LUKE 2:3–5

*T*his is the Silent Night, the Holy Night. The night
before Christmas when all through the house not a
creature is stirring. When the world in solemn
stillness lies to hear the angels sing.

Not in our house. Here everything's astir. We
have twelve overnight guests—four of them
unexpected—and the phone is ringing, and the
skirt I'm wearing to the midnight service has a
jammed zipper, and the callers at the door with gifts
are the ones I forgot to get anything for. And I'm
pressured and anxious and angry at myself for once
again failing to hear the angelic song. O little town

of Bethlehem, how still we see thee lie!

But isn't this part of the problem? That we've come to see Bethlehem this way over the centuries: that hushed and holy manger scene painted by artists? No doubt there was a hush in heaven that night; that is what artists with their gifted vision are showing us. But in Bethlehem I suspect it was more like pandemonium.

We have twelve extra people to house tonight; Bethlehem had additional hundreds. Could Mary and Joseph have been the only travelers lodged in that overflow space in the stable?

It's the unforeseen that upsets Christmas plans. But because of a sudden order from Rome, Mary's whole journey was unforeseen. How many painstaking preparations for the birth did she have to leave behind in Nazareth?

I chafe at crowded stores, but what about the press of people in those narrow streets? I've witnessed jostling, shouting market days in Israel— and those are willing crowds; two thousand years ago it would have been an angry one as well, herded together by order of a foreign dictator.

I'm distressed at what we've spent for Christmas. But I wonder—what was the price of bread in Bethlehem that night? How much did Joseph have to pay for the water Mary needed?

Silent night. Holy night. It was holy, of course, in the only place that matters—in the hearts of those who understood what was happening. But the holiness occurred in a noisy world. A time of history as tense and pressured as our own.

*Come, LORD JESUS, tonight, into this chaotic world of ours.*

77      *Christmas Day: All Paradox Resolved*

*And the Word became flesh.*
JOHN 1:14

*I*t's Christmas, the "Feast of Christ!" Time to open the stockings, unwrap the gifts, eat the holiday meal. After weeks of getting ready, today is the time awaited. Advent was the season of coming; Christmas is the season of arrival. Advent looked to the past and the future; Christmas celebrates the now.

We've watched for signs of His coming in the paradoxes of our lives. We looked for Him in our light but also in our darkness, in peace but also in pandemonium.

Today we experience Him as the great Resolver of all paradox. He is both Alpha and Omega, the first and the last. He is priest and sacrifice, servant and king, infant and Ancient of Days. He did not come to abolish the poles of our experience, our heights and our depths, but to unite them in himself, so that nothing that can happen to us, now or ever, will fall outside His all-inclusive providence.

*Paradox* is a Greek word meaning "contrary to expectation"—and how contrary to all preconceived ideas that first Christmas was! The Jews expected their Messiah to be a military conqueror; Jesus was born a carpenter's son. The Wise Men looked for Him at the court of the king; they found Him in a stable. Scholars foretold His birth; illiterate shepherds celebrated it.

His arrival is still like that: contrary to expectation. Today we meet Him not as we imagine Him to be, not as artists have painted Him nor saints extolled Him. But as we find Him in our own hearts at this moment, just as we are … with all our ambivalence, all our incompleteness … gathering all our contradictions into himself.

Merry Christmas! Merry, merry Christmas!

*Welcome, HOLY CHILD! Today You became man so that I could become a child of God.*